Tiger Lilies

Tiger Lilies

an American childhood

Fielding Dawson

Duke University Press

Durham, N.C.   1984

Portions of this volume previously appeared in
The Iowa Review, The Falcon, and as Sparrow 26
and Sparrow 49 published by Black Sparrow Press.

Printed in the United States of America on acid-free paper

Library of Congress Cataloging in Publication Data

Dawson, Fielding, 1930–
  Tiger lilies.

  1. Dawson, Fielding, 1930–   —Biography—Youth.
2. Authors, American—20th century—Biography.   I. Title.
PS3554.948Z477   1984   813'.54 [B]   84-4170
ISBN 0-8223-0593-3

ɔor's note

Certain manuscripts insist on being nothing less than the best, and—publication being a test of the art—the process equals the evidence: through the unnamed catalyst who submits the manuscript to the editor—David Southern, in this instance—with a telephone call out of the blue. Next, the best will not happen without a perceptive editor and copy-editor. Here, Joanne Ferguson and Anne Keyl. So it follows that there be a person to the author what the copy-editor is to the editor: in all forming one mind fixed in critical harmony on the text, with John Menapace's skilled layout and design, at hand. As I read the corrected, edited, and copy-edited manuscript aloud with Susan Maldovan— every word, every dot of punctuation—her ear, presence, often brilliant responses, awakened me to what I had written, and to what needed rewriting, which we did together. The hardest work there is, a story of its own, always. And always a rare one.

My thanks fail logic.

This is the third and final novel of a trilogy with no title. The first two works are *The Mandalay Dream* and *A Great Day for a Ballgame,* in that order. The streetcar accident only mentioned here is given due detail in *The Mandalay Dream.*

The initial star, invisible but to the author, is the typist. In this case Gerry Gilbert, who, in August 1976, in Vancouver, brought a detailed rough draft into the clean copy which served straight through to the page proofs, which

Susan and I read aloud, corrected anew, and went through again.

Warm thanks to John Dierkes for—in conversation—the Churchill quote regarding Edward R. Murrow, herein paraphrased.

FD

March 2, 1984
New York

Begin—soft.

Rolling in colors humming and singing to myself I felt something good, and crawling across silky softness to get as close as I could to what and where it was, I made my way sensing a structure.

A wonderful good radiated on me, good all around and I turned my face up, and closed my eyes in its soft and blinding goodness. I tried to stand up but fell down, so I sat and hummed and smiled to a horizontal crossing above my head and vertical shadows before me. Up and up I looked to the good, yet puzzled as it was softly untouchable. I opened my eyes, yet the goodness made me lower them, as it was good on and all around my face, through the structure as I happily smiled, happily puzzled.

The four of us were in the front seat, driving through the Everglades. Late at night. Daddy sang It's a long long way to Tipperary, on our way to The Land of Sunshine, 1934.

4

I sat on the beach and watched vultures eat the rotten corpse of the huge sea turtle.

They looked at me, and I edged back, a little further away, but not too far. Never.

I gazed out over the Atlantic. The sky was blue, and went forever. The ocean below, at my feet as I sat, was warm, and lapped at the sand. I waded, and then looked out, to the horizon.

What was out there?

Twenty yards to my left a breakwater made a long black line to the horizon, in an angle to a point of no vision, and I sat there on the sand, gazing out at it, into it, hypnotized by a distance beyond imagination, yet incredibly familiar, as the finite connection was made infinite the man in the sun and the star in the moon, the night in the day, and the day everywhere, warm, beautiful, wonderful Miami, collecting seashells with my sister Ca, against the great Atlantic.

Later (not much).

I looked out the window. In dawn's dim light I saw Freddy's house across the street. Freddy! Freddy was my friend.

We played with toy cars in the dirt at the side of my house, and when Daddy gave me the new truck with the trailer loaded with brightly painted cars, in the smell of lead and dry new paint rrrmmm ummm we unloaded cargo, and the little cars shifted gears on roads under construction on the side of the mountain.

Against all advice, while in Freddy's room on the second floor, we stuck our fingers into open sockets, and yelped in the shock.

I got out of bed, and quickly quietly put on my bunny slippers and my bathrobe, tiptoed into the hallway, and stopped. Mommy and Daddy were asleep, so was Ca, and I went down the steps, and holding the newel post, swung carefully to my right, and went down another smaller flight of steps into the living room, noticing the card table, loaded ashtrays and the cribbage board where they'd played.

I crossed the room, passing the sofa under which just before last Christmas I had discovered the Empire State Building, a sneaky one I'd been, in 1935 when I was five, in Pittsburgh, when Daddy had been sorry because he had wanted to give it to me because Ca and I had made blocks to stand bigger than him, but he had worked in the Empire State Building, and we had made our blocks stand taller than it!

I crossed over the spot where he and I played Kazan, *and* where the warm, soft, brown-skinned woman and I played bunny rabbit with my slippers when Mommy and Daddy went out, and she and I liked each other a lot. She put her

hand in one slipper and I put my hand in the other, and we
hopped around, and chased, and oh, oh I loved her affection,
and some nights her boyfriend visited her. He was
so BIG, my lips parted, and I looked up almost falling
over backwards to see the top of him, he was, he was
bigger than DADDY! and HE PICKED ME UP!—
and then he lowered me, and held me so that my face was
looking into his face, and my eyes widened, and I was
speechless in his large bright black face and I began,
I tried, I couldn't speak, and he jostled me, chuckled,
and said, softly,
     Heyoooo there!
     I burst into laughter, and—sparkled happiness as they
laughed, too, and then we all played, so whenever Mommy
and Daddy went out, and *she* came to be with me, I asked
her if *he* was coming, she was clever she was, because she
said Maybe, on some funny condition if I was *good*,
BUNNY RABBIT! I cried.
     On hands and knees on the rug, hopping around. Her
body beside mine.
     I opened the front door and slipped out opening the
screen door, and turning, with my back holding the screen
door, I closed the other door softly, and stepping out I
gently closed the screen door, walked to the edge of the
front porch, went down the steps and along the front walk
to the sidewalk, looked up and down the deserted street,
and went across, in silence and warm brightening dawn.
     Row on row, right and left, different sized and shaped
sleeping houses faced empty streets and yards. I walked
along Freddy's front walk, up his steps and onto his porch,
and knocked on his screen door to let 'em know I'd arrived,
and waited and gave it two raps, and after giving everyone
a fair chance, I rapped again because I was tired of waiting
when the door opened: Freddy's father looked down at me
through the screen door, a little grumpy, and clearing his

throat saying something about it being a little early? he belted his bathrobe tighter.

I looked up at him, and as I was about to ask if Freddy could come out and play, I was startled, and amazed, and angered that Freddy's father was so tall, so I said, with the surprise in my voice,

How come you're so much bigger'n me?

He said, sleepily, Because I'm older.

Not, I thought, what I meant.

I'm a man, he said, and you're a boy.

The hair on the back of my neck began to rise, someone was behind me, and in a half turn, my head and my gaze swung around to see a man standing in the middle of the street, looking at me. Our eyes met.

He stood erect and relaxed, hands at his sides, his pale almost bloodless face drawn, yet as if waiting, in a dark suit with an old-fashioned shirt unbuttoned at the collar, and no tie. He was rather shabby and yet it was as if he hovered there, shoes not quite on the asphalt, and his face, which was directly towards me, was yet as if in profile, for his left eye seemed to drill through his right, and as his face was narrow, and nose hardly visible, the way his lips blurred, he seemed amused, I saw a smile, and as his face was so opaque his black eyes seemed to be hollow circles, with red points in the middle, and I realized he knew me. He stood there, his eyes softly looking into my gaze, with his thin almost invisible lips smiling, yet then, not smiling at all, as he waited. A breeze crossed my forehead, grazed my ear and curled down my neck and around down across my naked chest under my pajama top and bathrobe and I blinked in a shudder at the empty street, turned to Freddy's father, and not knowing what to say, asked,

Can Freddy come out and play?

In my little voice. I smiled, and his father said Fee, it's too early, can you come back later?

I nodded, and apologized as he backed inside and closed the door. I went down the steps, and crossed the spot where the stranger in dark clothes had been, and returned to my room the way I had come. I took off my bathrobe and bunny slippers, climbed into bed and pulled the covers up, and wondered and wondered, and taking one of my most favorite Big Little Books, *Tiny Tim and the Mechanical Men,* from off the shelf, I read until the sun was up and I was asleep.

Mommy was foxy, like Reynard. She put her beautiful face into mine, and with a laughing wicked look in her eyes, she grabbed me, clicked her teeth, and said in her throat,

I *gotcha!*

Then embraced me. I spun all the way up to the sky, in a laugh in her arms mmmmmaa.

My girlfriend's name was Ingrid, and her mother was a Swedish opera singer. Their living room was dark. It had a lot of rugs, big and little statues, tasseled lamps, paintings, mirrors, books, and record albums, with the player in a corner. Their front porch was small, and in twilight we sat on the rail, held hands, and once I kissed her. She was beautiful. Blonde, and her hair in ringlets.

Her mother was beautiful too.

Long blonde pigtails, and full-breasted like Mommy. But bigger, with dresses of many colors.

One afternoon I was lying naked on my back on Mommy's bed. She was putting on my socks when she saw I was stiff. She laughed, and playfully touched me before she put on my underpants, mm.

Mr. Smith was fat and funny. One of the other boarders. He was a joker, and did funny things that embarrassed Mommy like leaving fake dog crap in unusual places, just inside the door, etc., where nobody could miss it, and when Mommy saw it and was angry and then laughed and kicked it out the door into the hallway there was Mr. Smith and he picked it up, put it in his pocket, and walked down the hallway a big grin.

Mother said, That *man.*

In the evenings the Blaney brothers, who were the landlady's sons, gathered around the piano and sang. Jack had a wonderful voice, and when he sang "Stairway to the Stars," my sister looked at him, and her eyes got kinda misty. I think she had a crush on him. I was six.

She was eleven.

We'll build a stairway to the stars, Jack sang, and looked at her with a smile, and after meeting his gaze, she lowered her eyes.

She had a crush on him all right.

He was sixteen.

In the first grade the other boys were so much bigger, and especially the colored kids, boy they were so big, and so *fast*, and so frightening. I stayed out of their way.

Coming home some of the neighborhood kids saw me. They were standing in an empty lot, were older, and bigger, and they had a blanket. I didn't know them, except by sight, and I thought they were Irish. They invited me to play with them, and when I got there, they put me in the blanket, and as each one held a corner, they threw me into the air which terrified me and I began to cry, begging them to stop, but they wouldn't, and threw me higher, when suddenly they let me down, hard. I turned to see why, and my sister was running across the lot shouting at them to let me go, saying they'd *better* let me go, or—they did, too, and they ran.

She knelt down in front of me, and her angry eyes softened,

You're all right, aren't you?

I nodded, and put my arms around her. I put my head on her shoulder and wept. She said, as she embraced me,

Oh sweet heart.

Steep hills, long streets, coal dust everywhere, under low overcast skies, except on some days.

A torn election poster for Alf Landon.

A woman in a green dress with pearls at her throat, and bobbed light brown hair. She is smoking a Lucky Strike cigarette at the wheel of a blue roadster. White wall tires. She smiles to us.

Tiger Lilies

In Memory of Arthur Lefford

who said: "Write it."

"...nothing ever wipes out childhood."

Simone de Beauvoir, *A Very Easy Death*

A capital ship for an ocean trip
Was the *Walloping Window Blind*—
No gale that blew dismayed her crew
Or troubled the captain's mind.
The man at the wheel was taught to feel
Contempt for the wildest blow.
And it often appeared, when the weather had
    cleared,
That he'd been in his bunk below.

So, blow ye winds heigh ho
A-roving I will go.
I'll stay no more on England's shore
So let the music play—ay—ay,
I'm off for the morning train,
I'll cross the raging main,
I'm off to my love with a boxing glove
Ten thousand miles away.

Charles Edward Carryl, *Davy and the Goblin:
A Nautical Ballad*

After we had stopped in Grand Rapids, which was after
we had left Muddy Run and we'd returned to Blairsville,
we went to live for good in Kirkwood, Missouri.
Grandfather had died there in 1936, and we'd gone home
for the funeral, so I'd been in Kirkwood before. But in the
spring of, I think 1938, our car pulled to a stop and my
Aunty Mary ran across the lawn to welcome us with cries
of You're here at last! Well! Well, here at last! Warm hugs
and kisses, and an invitation to Come in! Come on in!
Which with our bags and suitcases, we did.

I spent the first day or two meeting and looking at my
four aunts and my Uncle Essex (who was only a little
bigger'n me, and whose room I was going to share and who
I loved immediately). I prowled around the room, it had
three walls of books, a potbellied stove, and two windows
both with a view.

Then I investigated the house, with its back stairs and
dark basement, and then I wandered around the yard:
looking across the street.

I walked down my sidewalk. I stopped and stood, in
short pants and my favorite blue pullover, my socks kind of
bagged a little, and my shoes were scuffed, but I wasn't
thinking of anything except some kids across the street,
who were playing, and whom I didn't know. I was seven
years old.

Well, occasionally they glanced across at me, and then
went on playing.

Their game took them a little farther down the street,
and I followed them on my side, watching them, and then
one of them looked across at me, and said,

Aren't you new here?

I nodded, and shy to speak, I finally cried,
Yes! My name's Fee Dawson! Will you let me play with
you?

I met the Lizard and his brother Wimp and their sister Cecily (Cissie), and I met Steve and his brother Hobey and their sister Jan, and I met Gary: and Joe and his brother Jim who was little, and had bright red hair, and as the days went by I met their parents, and their parents met me and I got to know everyone, and their houses and yards and I found some secret places in such a way I could feel secret in the finding and then in the constant feeling even if I was in an obvious place (a creek) I was at home with mystery, and above all, happily willing, with enthusiasm to be mystified anywhere there was a chance to feel the suspense in doing new things.

I kept my eyes open. We played a lot of games.

Twilight!

I raced across the Lizard's back yard, and after a long jump, rolled under the grapevines, and trying to control my breathing, I dug in the soft cool dirt, and lay gazing across the darkening lawn. He was out there, waiting, and my heart beat fast.

I heard somebody scream, and I laughed, and then somebody else laughed—but a soft laugh, right near me! I felt a hand on my hand, and I turned my head just as I smelled the gentle milk-pith girlsmell, with a whiff of sneaker, she whispered, very very softly:

Fee.

It was Cissie!

I whispered: *Yes!* and she was silent. Me too.

Tense and bright-eyed we lay holding hands under the grapevines, in the sound of crickets, and winking fireflies, in June, 1940. Night excitement. Kick the can.

We were playing guns, and I was hiding in some bushes by the barn in Steve's yard, when he crept up to me, and said, Hey, in low, tense words:

The Japanese have just bombed Pearl Harbor.

The Japanese! I cried.

He nodded. Dad called Mother from his office, and told her.

I said, But what does it mean? Why did they?

I don't know. Mom said Dad said President Roosevelt will go to Congress to ask for a Declaration of War.

The Lizard, Wimp, and their two sisters Cissie and baby Butch lived in a large white house with dark green shutters, set amid trees about a hundred feet back from the tree-lined street (called Taylor Avenue), four houses down from where I lived, on the other side.

Their house was really big: three stories, just under mansion size, and had an open porch on the left which faced the driveway, and a porch on the right side (where we played Monopoly) which was almost all windows and faced Gary's house. Lizard's front door, with a little semicircle window above it, was set squarely in the middle of the house, which faced the street.

There was a fourth floor: dark rooms with low ceilings. Storerooms.

The basement was large, and served as laundry, playroom, and workshop. The laundry was a real one, and so was the workshop. So was the playroom, dominated by a wonderful pingpong table, amid boxes of blocks and toys beneath casement windows. But the ceiling was low, so we learned to keep our slams down. But all the ceilings in the other rooms: the first three floors, were high, and the rooms plushly decorated, especially the living room and the dining room, with thick Oriental rugs and low glass-doored bookcases with vases and statues on top, and with an easy chair and an ottoman here and there, and the big sofa and low coffee table across from the fireplace it kind of looked like a club.

The Lizard's father was an executive for Socony-Vacuum, and he took care of his house and yard that way: conservative, and careful, the first person I ever met who talked to trees. I mean he let them know when they weren't earning their living.

His first name was Jeff, and he was tall, thin, a little gaunt, had a ready smile and wore neat stiff suits to work, the bow tie type, hat and topcoat, and on occasions he thought were big, for example if it was his turn to pass out the leaflets in church on Sundays, or to take the collection, he wore tails and striped pants, and I remember my mother saying afterwards, to my Aunty Katie, that Jeff was in his tails this morning, in her striped pants peal of laughter. There were several men in our parish and neighborhood who were as wealthy as Lizard's father, but they never wore stripes and tails, and for once the laughter was shared by kids and their folks alike because if Jeff was at church and looked like he was at a funeral, well, what else but laugh? His wife, Lizard's mother, never knew the diff, hand on his arm as they entered the pew. She was a good size woman, the adults called her plump and we saw it fat: we laughed (she wasn't funny), and they didn't. Her looks fooled you. Her face was round and pleasant, she had bobbed light brown hair, good shoulders, a loaded chest, and a wide waist. Her ankles were slender and she had a fast mean temper with a voice that sent us head over heels out of her house, if she wanted it that way. I mean, if it was a nice day and we were in the basement playing pingpong, she'd want us outside, and we went, or about fifteen minutes before supper, she'd open the door to the basement and call out our names beginning with the Lizard and Wimp, Cissie and Marjorie (Butch) wash up for supper and the rest of us go HOME.

Boy, Mom, Lizard's mother sure has a voice!

My mother laughed. No hanky-panky *there:* not like here where you can get away with it.

Yeah, well I'm glad you don't yell at me like that, I pouted.

Did Mother think maybe she should? When I really

made her angry? No. She was also thinking she was glad, too: she didn't want to be like that woman at all, and I puzzled at how adults could know each other and it wouldn't matter except when it did.

I laughed. Plus Lizard's dad!

Mother laughed with me, and repeated, Plus Jeff! You're *such* a wonderful boy!

I lowered my eyes and smiled. Not that I was wonderful, although I admit I had my moments, I wondered how she could get that out of that and I was puzzled. in my wonderfulness. But she liked to laugh, and was happy when she did. Even so I frowned. Even as we laughed together, which she liked best of all. She asked:

Why do you frown when I tell you you're wonderful?

I don't know.

I've embarrassed you? Made you self-conscious, that's it. Well, even if *you* don't think you're wonderful: *I* do, so go ahead out and play. I'll call you when supper's ready.

I didn't want to disappoint her! Where were the words? I wished my father would come home.

You write me, I'd written to him: in New York.

I wandered in the yard and then Mother called and I went inside, washed my hands, and went into the dining room for supper.

The next day I walked down the street to see the Lizard. The back door to his house, from which we made our sudden exits, was also the door we used to enter. Not the front door. The front door was for company.

The back door opened into the kitchen from a small sheltered cement-floored porch, and it was this door we used, and Hattie, their maid, who was a steady ninety degrees hotter in temper than Lizard's mother and just about twice her size, though built along the same lines and in fact if Hattie wasn't so black, and didn't shuffle when she walked, in a glance you couldn't tell 'em apart, though Hattie had the edge in voice: hers'd flatten a Leacock hardball, and in a way of impression we saw a single figure. If any of their kids came home late, or tracked mud across Hattie's clean kitchen floor and then ran into Hattie, or Lizard's mother or both—as the rest of us stood outside, the walls of the house seemed to bulge, and in little puffs of smoke, with lines behind them, we heard a sudden third voice, weeping, as we crept away thanking God we didn't live in that house: we watched as the Lizard picked and then ate his scabs, licked snot off his finger, and when jarred in football, he fell, writhed, and groaned and cried. . . .

But in Sunday school or church everything that had gone on during the week fell into its proper irregular forgotten place and the kids and their families prayed and sang together, and during Lent reluctantly contributed to our mite boxes, and in the winters while listening to the sermon wanting to get on our sleds, and in the summer to play ball, we partook of the Body and Blood of our Lord Jesus Christ, and the Lizard's father imagined a large family lunch with nobody invited but them. That's not fair to say that, in a way, but in a way it is. They weren't selfish people, but they sure could be cheap about things that didn't matter to them, and mattered a lot to us. Or vice versa. It was, anyway, on those Sunday kind of days off in the summer, when Lizard's father got away from his job, that I was most interested in him. The way he puttered around in the yard. I mean in his way of doing what he wanted to and make it right: wrong was a word he didn't know, and to do something was to do it right, or, as he said, don't do it at all, and we stood around agreeing, having fixed our faces to look agreeable, which he liked: at last showing intelligence because, which he didn't mention, we were listening to him, which we appeared to be doing, but. . . . One day, as we crossed their front yard on the way to Matthews' Field to play some Indian ball, near the mail box by the street we saw Lizard's father, standing staring at a small tree, his lips

moving, but his figure still: in faded green and white
pin-striped work pants, worn white shirt, and canvas
sneakers. We stopped, and I got that certain feeling. I looked
at the man and the kids looked at me. Go on, they began,
ask him: do it again. *Ask him*. They were laughing and my
eyes were bright, as Mac, or Steve, or Gene who *wanted* to
belong, shoved me a little, saying quietly, *Do it again,* as the
Lizard, Wimp, and Cissie controlled themselves, frowning
and frightened standing with their hands at their sides, and
staring at their father, it was all of us with gloves, bats, and
balls, looking at the man as I slowly approached him, and in
my short pants, stood beside him, watching him take a Boy
Scout hatchet, and, holding the small tree by the trunk,
chop it down.

I said hello to him.

He looked up. Why hello, Fielding.

I pointed to the felled tree, aware of the kids behind me,
near collapse from stifled laughter, and I said, all choirboy,

Why did you chop down that tree?

He looked up at me as he knelt by the tree, and said,
firmly,

Because, Fielding, this tree (he pointed) did not earn its
living: and a dozen kids collapsed on the grass. I grinned
and backed away saying Thanks, I had wondered—

I did it again and again! Same question and got the same
answer that touched off the same outburst in the others,
and Lizard's father never even wondered why, it seemed,
although he generally made a small white smile.

Once in a while, when we were bored, somebody would
use that line, tackle somebody else in a living room and say
You aren't earning your living! to our answering cries of
delight.

One afternoon the Lizard's father became weary of
digging dandelions, their big yard—front, back, and side
—was loaded with 'em, and he told Wimp and the Lizard
he'd pay a penny for every ten dandelions they could get,

so they got hold of the gang, and (knowing better), we each got a bushel basket and went to work. A couple of hours later the yard had been picked clean and we came in with around seventeen thousand dandelions, and just at the sight the Lizard's father went pale. We emptied our baskets and each began a count, but he said no as we made little bunches of tens, You misunderstood me. I said (he said), a penny for every *hundred,* and Wimp said, No, Father, it was a penny for every ten, and his father said, No, no, That's too—you've misunder—it's a penny for every hundred and even if I had said it, which I didn't, it was foolish for you children to expect so much money, asking us to consider: think, he said: dandelions, dug up in a quantity that *I* would say worth real cash? Dandelions? Think, boys, think, he smiled: look, he said, at all those weeds. Then he laughed. A ha ha ha, ha.

We nodded, You're right, as usual, sir, they're just weeds: but labor isn't.

"Why do you think we did it?" Hobey asked. He was the oldest.

Wimp began to whimper, as his father made a generous laugh, the Ha ha type again, and said, Yes, that's true, and so as your work won't have been for nothing, here's a little something for each of you, and he gave each of us a dime.

Aw gee whiz, we said.

The effect on Wimp and the Lizard was grim, and as we walked away we grumbled some, but we were forced to defer to the Lizard's and Wimp's shame, and their disappointment in their father, as Wimp repeated He said a penny for every *ten,* he did! and we knew it because it fit: that's what he would do, and later lie to suit himself—to fit what was right to him, for him, even in little things. Which were big to us: it was the money, but more than that it was the way he had with it, and as we walked across the clean yard, and out onto Taylor Avenue and down to Kirkwood for some ice cream, having a clue to a generous adult's cheapskate character, the ice cream looked good but he'd broken his word. We were all liars, I was anyway, so could understand, but he had lied about our money, and although everybody lied about money, we didn't have any to lie about and he did so he could, and somehow that was serious: it gave him the power, it gave him the right to lie. So that lie belonged to him as much as his pants, shirt, and sneakers. I mean, other people had money too, but when the Lizard's father on a ten-dandelions-for-a-penny deal lied, that lie belonged to him in a complicated way that was right to him, for him, and to us was wrong: more than meets the eye: from ten to a hundred, in others words it went from us to him: all those dandelions for a dollar twenty.

At supper I said I had collected 556 dandelions, that's 56 cents, and Hobey had over 700.

Oh Jeff's such a cheapskate, Mother said. Uncle Mouse (Essex) said, smiled, rather, You kids oughta go on strike.

We all laughed, and the next day I told the gang what Mouse had said, and for the rest of the summer whenever Lizard's father got that I'd like you boys to do a little chore look, we said we were on strike and walked away from him, which meant it fell on the Lizard, Wimp, and Cissie and that wasn't so funny because it meant we were three short until they got the chore done. But the Lizard's father had laughed, at first, too, when we said we were on strike.

He knew what a strike was.

One night Wimp and Lizard invited me for supper: I'd never been before, and I was curious how they did it. Apprehensive, too. I was surprised when their mother and father said it was okay, but when I showed up, it was at the back door.

Then, there we were at the table, and sitting down. Hattie brought out the tomato juice and the aspic and I liked aspic like I liked okra, which I hated, and after Wimp's father said grace, I dabbled around the jelly with my fork, and watched everybody eat theirs right off. The Lizard's father sat at the head of the table, and made a joke about how to make a jam sandwich, you get two slices of bread, butter one slice, put jelly on the other, and jam 'em together, get it? The kids winced and their mother stayed silent: nobody said anything so I didn't either. I spread my aspic around the lettuce leaf so it looked like I'd eaten some, and finally Hattie cleared it away. Then she brought the main dish out. The Lizard, Wimp, Cissie, and even the baby, Butch, groaned: my empty stomach sank as Hattie put the platter of liver in front of Wimp's father who said, in a warning tone, something about it being good for us. The Lizard's face was crimson, and his head was down: Wimp was whimpering and Cissie's pretty face was bleached. As I received my plate I closed my eyes, it was so awful.

At home when we had liver Mother said if I ate a couple of bites it would be all right. She didn't force me, and I was able, by mixing a lot of mashed potatoes and pepper and oleo, to get a couple of bites down, but that night at the Lizard's it wasn't a small slice like I got at home, it was a hunk about the size of my foot, nicely fixed up, I'll admit, with a slice of bacon around it, and the toothpick in there, anybody could see this was really good liver and there was Wimp sitting there next to me with tears in his eyes and his father lecturing about essential vitamins and I almost threw up from the smell as the other kids were squirming in their chairs saying aw aw aw *gee,* who can, aw Dad, gee Mom, but nothing doing, they *had* to eat that liver, and it was then while I was enjoying the mashed potatoes and string beans which were swell, like the bread and butter, that I saw their cocker spaniel pad into the dining room and begin to wag his tail at Wimp's leg: I looked at Wimp who looked at me. Wimp wore big round glasses which made his eyes look bigger, and we looked at each other. I glanced around the table, and as nobody was looking I coolly slid the hot liver off the plate into my left hand and dropped it onto the Oriental rug, and the dog ate it up, Wimp and me were in near hysterics, that dog really *loved* liver, and Wimp who was laughing so hard it looked like he was crying, nothing new, slid his liver onto the rug, too, and when his father looked our way and saw our clean plates, he made a little speech, about virtue, or something, I saw I had come a little ways in his eyes and I felt sort of adult: I smiled: blushed: faked and faked and faked and the Lizard and Cissie were biting their lips fiercely, and picking around their liver as the dog walked out of the room so full of liver it was almost coming out of his mouth, he almost stumbled off the edge of the rug—and there was the rest of Wimp's liver on the rug! Five feet beyond the table and Wimp looked at me, I looked at him: we looked at each other not knowing whether to laugh or cry, what could we do? get up, get the meat and put it in our pocket, return to the table, sit down and—etc., sooooo we pretended it wasn't there! What liver? and I had another piece of bread and butter and looked at the dog, who had fallen by the sofa in the living room, and I looked at the hunk of unfinished liver on the rug, and at Wimp who was perspiring, and then supper was over, and we were sitting in the living room when Wimp's mother saw the liver on the rug, and faked a heart attack.

Wimp and me, the Lizard, and Cissie, stood there big-eyed, mouths open. Who did—how did that liver get on the rug? gee WHIZ!

Well. Well; well: there it was, just as we, at the foot of Wimp's mother and father, tall cleanshaven skyscrapers: powerful perfume ruffles inquired if that was my liver on her Oriental rug? No, I said, in the terrific suspense I loved more than anything, little wings fluttering, and she looked at Wimp and raised her hand, my eyes widened *oh no,* and Wimp began to cry and cringe, she took a step forward, his head was down a little and his eyes were raised, her eyes blazed fury and she hit him so hard his glasses flew: screaming at him, that he go to his room *this* instant. Cissie found his glasses, and gave them to him, and he crossed the room rubbing behind his ear, and really weeping, deeply sobbing.

His brother and sister were drawn and terrified: their mother was ready to spring, and nobody moved. With her violent voice she whipped Wimp up the stairs to bed, and as Wimp got to the top of the stairs, he turned, I mean he had to, he pointed at me, and sobbed his double cross:

It was Fee who—who started it!

I was never thrown out of a house so fast. The front door. They had turned on me: I had ruined their rug. Was that my liver? No. Where, then, *was* my liver? The dog ate it. So Wimp had gotten the idea—Yes, it's my fault, I admitted, and backed away from them feeling a breeze on my neck because I was on the front porch with the slammed door in my face.

I stood a second. The streetlight shone through the trees at the end of the walk. It was peaceful, even beautiful. Unreal.

I walked home feeling depressed for Wimp, and me too, my head full of her screaming about her ruined rug, and when I got home Mother asked me how it had gone, and I told her. She lowered her eyes:

Aw, Fee, you shouldn't have, and she shook her head saying, You *know* how they are: poor Wimp, it's going to be days.

I nodded and said I was sorry. I went into my room to see if I could do something good, like homework, for a change, ha ha, and about a half an hour later, reading *Air Trails*, I heard my Aunty Dot laugh, and cry,

Oh, he *didn't* (high pitched)—the dog!

Shhhh, he'll hear you.

I don't care. You know how he hates liver. All children do. Why did they serve it? Oh! so foolish—well, the dog. Boy I'll bet Jeff blew his top.

I heard Mother laugh, and then they both laughed, and as they walked away, laughter diminished: like at the theater.

That weekend while I watched Uncle Mouse fool with his home-made camera, he looked up at me through the smoke of a Wings cigarette, and said, in that slow not quite whispery I've-seen-it-all voice I loved so much,

I didn't know dogs liked their liver hot.

I put my arms around him, which embarrassed him, and I said,

I didn't either, but *that* dog does!

Yeah, he said, and laughed softly, and you found out the hard way. You and Wimp.

Me and Wimp, I agreed, sadly. With a smile.

The Lizard was swell the way he could build flying models so fast. It took me days. And also wooden toy guns. He worked—so did we all if we needed toys—in his basement workshop: we made almost all the toys we used everyday, ourselves. Once Joey, who joined our gang later on, and he was younger than we were, once he didn't have a gun (we didn't call it cops and robbers, we called it *guns*), and the Lizard on the jigsaw cut one out, sanded and painted it, and like his father, offered it to Joey for two bits and because we were all so anxious to play guns, Joey bought it: pretty bitterly. Why didn't the Lizard give it to him?

You live just across the field, why don't you go home and get one? said the Lizard.

Joey began to cry and said it wasn't fair.

Later on that day, after we'd played a lot and were tired BAM you're *dead*, you ARE! the Lizard told Joey he was a sap to have bought it.

It took about five minutes for the paint to dry, and while you were waiting around you could have gone home and—

Joey made a face, and was about to cry and we laughed. What a sap!

In the Lizard's back yard, near the driveway that led to Steve's house, and which also turned off to Gary's house, there was an old chicken house that was our clubhouse. Just behind it was the tree where we had our tree house, from which some of us fell, especially the Lizard, he had

a lot of scars and he ate a lot of scabs and pus before
they healed. Once I fell out of the tree house, and was
almost seriously hurt.

A kind of cracked sidewalk separated the chicken
house and the tree from a toolshed that was in the shape of
a barn, a small barn, and as the sidewalk ran in front of the
toolshed, it became the crest of a small dirt cliff with a
ditch at the base that extended to the driveway. We made
little furnaces in the ditch, and pretended to forge iron and
steel—the summer after Pearl Harbor—two years before
the Lizard, Wimp, Cissie, Butch, and their mom and dad
moved to Long Island in New York—but two years before,
we played a lot of *planes,* and no matter who was on which
side, the furnaces became major targets. We built solid
model U.S., German, English, and Japanese planes, holding
them at arm's length with the tips of our fingers, we flew
our missions and had our dogfights. By wetting the tip of a
kitchen match and lighting it, and holding it against the
cowling, the smoke and sputtering flame left a trail against
the sky as we got shot down. It was fun to get shot down,
and wait in the jungle grass beside my Spitfire as Steve and
his Dinky Toy weapons carrier came across Matthews'
jungle Field to rescue me.

Matthews' Field was north of the tennis court, south
of which was Matthews' Pool, which was right next to the
two-car garage where Lizard's father and mother each had
a car. Behind the garage and across the back yard was the
fence along where Steve and Hobey and Jan lived in a
modern one-story house: their property was about an acre
and a half, and on the farthest eastern edge the 01 streetcar
tracks crossed a bridge that crossed a creek, and at the
point where the high dirt banks flanked the creek as it went
under the bridge, was a landing field: another major target,
so the air raids went from the creek by the tracks westward
to the blast furnaces, across the Lizard's back yard on
an angle across the driveway and north along the tennis

court and across Matthews' Field to the northwestern corner where Taylor Avenue met Bodley (Joey lived on Bodley): High Command for whichever country we decided should be there, but it was generally involved with the English Tank Corps, and there was a lot of artillery. Exactly across the length of the field, near Matthews' Barn, where Old Gus milked cows and fascinated us by sharpening sickles and knives and axes, near the apple trees and the grape arbor, was, Nazi headquarters, which had to change location because Mr. Matthews didn't like our digging up his grass, and said it was okay if they, the Nazis, could move to a spot alongside the tennis court if we stayed off the court itself, which we did, with difficulty, as that court looked like the Sahara Desert to us, and to think of the great tank wars simply across a white chalk line, was almost too painful to bear. Mr. Matthews didn't allow us to do any definitive digging, so we made little hangars and gun emplacements out of sticks above ground, and they worked all right, although it was great to really make an airport. But as we changed sides every day from Jap to English to Nazi to the U.S., we each got a chance to use the field by the tracks, and that was a terrific spot, especially from so far away.

My FW190 came in low under the apple trees and the Wimp yelled CHEERIO HERE THEY COME! and cranked up the antiaircraft guns: as I came over dropping my sticks I got hit and banking right away from the tennis court wetting a match, my plane began smoking and from across the field I saw the Lizard coming at me in a Spitfire, and as my plane lost altitude, the Lizard, seeing me going down looking for a place to land, came in and around behind me for the kill as I crash landed and Steve appeared in an ME109, and momentarily frightened the Spitfire away, and covered my landing: he then banked up with the Lizard following him as Hobey in his ME109 showed up and Lizard made a pretty close right-angled turn. Steve stopped, and holding the plane in his hand, said, You can't do that.

Why can't I? (He knew)

Because you wouldn't know if I would bank, and also planes can't make sharp turns like that.

You had to bank, the Lizard said, the Spitfire is faster than the ME109, and—

True, but you couldn't know which *way* I'd bank, and you would've gone straight by me, Steve said.

That's TRUE! I yelled.

In passion to keep on playing the Lizard agreed and Steve resumed his bank, the Lizard went on by and Hobey followed him, whereupon Steve banked, and as soon as he was on the Lizard's Spitfire's tail, the Spitfire banked to the left and, true to his word, Steve kept on going, and Hobey's ME109 banked left and shot the Lizard down NO YOU DIDN'T he yelled as Hobey stood there. The Lizard's Spitfire kept on going and Hobey and Steve and me looked at each other: he doesn't even know how to *play*, he doesn't know which planes fly how, though we knew better. So did the Lizard. But he could want things his way.

Occasionally a new kid showed up and we had to explain the rules. We had read a lot of books and magazines and newspaper articles on the planes. We knew how to build them to scale and we knew the statistics: the FW190 had short range, but heavy firepower, it was my favorite plane because the cowling was yellow and it belonged to the enemy —with whom I invariably identified—and it was built like I wanted to be: stocky, with a lot of firepower. Also, I thought the pants on the retractable landing gear were prrretty neat, and the way the Germans painted the cross on the fuselage and wings was terrific: we could all draw, and we could draw all the planes, from any angle (in shop at school, later, we took aircraft spotter training seriously, hoping some nifty day we'd see a gang of Stukas buzz Kirkwood—we'd spot 'em), and anyway, when the new kid showed up and made a 90-degree bank, no matter how he complained we told him he couldn't do that, like when planes slow they don't suddenly go right down, they slant first, etc., he couldn't do it his way because his way wasn't real, and the planes were real and if he said something like,

Aw it's just a game,

Hobey said, That's true, but this is our game, we build our planes and our landing fields, and when you play with us you play our way.

How do you play?

We play real.

The Lizard, the wizard building guns and model airplanes, also made model trains and even the tracks, and one afternoon when inspired, he made a long balsawood trestle that led from the sidewalk in front of the toolshed, out over the ditch past the chicken house and almost to the driveway —beyond the blast furnaces. Then he built a low inclining track across the sidewalk to join with the track on the trestle: a train track and trestle in miniature, about eighteen inches up from the bottom of the gulley, and all told, about twelve feet long.

Then he made the train. An engine, coal car, a couple of freight cars (loaded with kitchen matches), and a caboose. It had taken him all day, and that evening after supper we all gathered around in twilight by the light from the blast furnaces, and while getting ourselves dizzy from blowing them up to blast pitch, the Lizard placed about twenty firecrackers at certain places on the train, and after making sure the wheels would turn and the train would go when he pushed it, he poured half a pint of gasoline over the train, track, and trestle as we circled around breathless, some of us squatting Indian-fashion on the sidewalk and in the dirt, with wood smoke and summer and fireworks in our heads, like a magician in a hurry the Lizard lit the trestle, and in a leap gave the train a gentle push, and set it downward going.

The trestle burst into flame, and the train, as it came down the grade and then onto the trestle caught fire, and in the inferno, kept on going, as every part of the balsa trestle burned, and as the train reached the middle the trestle began to sag as we yelled and danced and clapped in glee —kaWHAM:CRACK in a series of explosions the trestle simultaneously with the train: blasted everywhere, *all* of it to smithereens as we jumped back, cheering, fire in our eyes as the mad Lizard danced and waved his hands and we slapped him on the back.

Fireworks!

And in the afternoons, we begged him to make the Moth, and blow it up midair: the trick of tricks! : fireworks in the sky!

He had done it often, it was always the Curtis Moth, a flying model with rubber band engine, and as it was a pain in the ass to make, especially as the Lizard could be so moody, he often gave in, and disappeared into his house and into the basement with the gang of us on his heels willing to do anything to speed up construction. His hands worked in a blur as he laid out the wings, the fuselage, the stabilizers, and the rudder, there was little we could do, but we did as we could: Hobey and Steve glued parts together and the rest of us cut the tissue paper to cover it, and after about an hour and a half, it was finished. We didn't bother sprinkling it with water to make the tissue drumtight, but we gazed over his shoulder fascinated as he placed the firecrackers in along the fuselage and inside behind the cowling, and then tested it there, to see if it flew on a straight and balanced line, and if it didn't he'd make it so it did, and everybody except the Lizard went outside and stood in the back yard near the tree house tree, but more toward the center of the yard, and waited, gazing up at the fourth floor.

A window opened. We saw the Lizard's head and hand

as he waved, which meant that with a gasoline soaked plane
with a wingspan of about two feet, and loaded with
firecrackers, he'd made his way up from the basement to the
fourth floor missing Hattie and his mother, a dangerous
journey, and we saw him fiddle with the plane, wind up the
propeller, and with a kitchen match, light the cowling
— WHFF the plane in flames out it came on his soft throw
on a rise against the blue sky: what a sight! A plane on
fire, and just over the old apple tree behind the back porch,
the first firecracker went off and we cheered, and with its
fuselage shattered the cracker in the cowling went and the
broken plane began its descent, as in a double blast the
wing was gone, too, then the tail section went to bits,
the fuselage completely blew apart, and in a dying flaming
raggedy shambles the debris tumbled to the ground as we
jumped and waved our hands as the Lizard, breathless,
joined us at the last moment to witness the end of his
art with a big grin, and we surrounded him shouting and
cheering. It had been a close call, he said: his mother
had been sewing in her room, and Hattie was dusting
just inside the doorway, but he had made it by, and we saw
the fear on his face. We went to the chicken house for a
smoke, and sat on boxes or on the floor behind burlap-
covered windows, which unbeknown to us, the smoke
curled through, even adults could see, and we made
plans for a bigger plane that Lizard could glue *two-inchers*
to—a B17!—we howled, rolling on the floor seeing
that four-engine bomber go to bits in the sky! And later
that night, at home, I listened to the radio and the
war news with my Aunty Dot and my sister: we heard
Edward R. Murrow from London, and the bombs falling,
and that night I could hardly sleep for the impending
excitement of the Lizard and tomorrow.
   Two-inchers!
   Tomorrow!

The Fog Comes In

When my Uncle Charley came to visit, he came whirling in touching everyone and thing in his path, beginning when his old mud-splattered banged-up truck squeaked, shuddered, and jolted to a stop by the bushes at the end of the front walk. And his thin wife Eloise with the baby girl Serena in her arms climbed out of the front seat, and Charley himself angled out from behind the wheel, yelling at his other three daughters in back, who from behind slatted side braces peeped and steadily gazed at the house where I lived. Betty, the oldest and my sister's age. Cathy and Mary Lou came next—a few years younger than Betty though several years in front of Serena, and they all climbed out of the back of the truck, and laughing shyly, walked up the walk big-eyed behind their father and mother. They were all poorly dressed, but their different faces were as clear as an invasion force, fresh in from the farm.

They thundered up the front steps, the three girls almost blushing with curiosity, but to me they were also a threat, they came through my new but accumulating self-fog as if they didn't see it, or even their own fog, and our house shifted and shook when Charley banged on the front door, opened it himself, and came in shouting, he had a natural shout, and a special greeting: his voice jumped around books, paintings, the upright piano, and horsehair stuffed furniture in my Victorian house: DARATHY! KERRA! MARY! KATIE! MILDRED! ESSEX! *I'M HERE WITH ELOISE AND THE GIRLS—*

Aunty Mil—Why it's *Charley!*

Aunty Katie, putting down *The Saturday Evening Post,* and with an effort, rising from the pillows on the swing in the little screened-in cabin, covered with morning glories in the back of the main house, saying to herself softly, in the fall of feet and murmurs, gee whiz, Daddy? golly, boy!

Well, I'd better get Mary to make some sandwiches. Charley's here.

As she left the little building, I heard Mother say, Dorothy, Charley's here—with Eloise and the kids.

Oh? Good! Dorothy cried. I was sure it would be today.

Mother and Aunty Dot came downstairs just behind Mildred, Mother saying,

We'd better get Mary to make some sandwiches. The kids will be hungry.

Aunty Mary was on her hands and knees in the garden, in among the roses, in fact, pulling weeds, and Aunty Katie crossed the back lawn, and when she was just behind her sister, called—loud, 'cause Aunty Mary was deaf,

MARY! CHARLEY'S HERE WITH ELOISE AND THE KIDS!

Aunty Mary went on pulling weeds.

MARY!

She had unplugged her hearing aid. Katie tapped her on the shoulder.

—MARY!

Aunty Mary looked up, startled, and Aunty Katie said, patiently, as Aunty Mary fiddled with the hearing device,

Mary, Charley's here with Eloise and the kids, come in and make some *sandwiches!*

Aunty Mary's face was puzzled as she got the parts connected, tuned up and in, and then she looked up, making little sounds in her throat, she had a guitar in her throat, and with a warm expression and bright eyes, she said,

Charley's here?

Katie smiled and nodded, and said something about sandwiches. Aunty Mary's face clouded, but then she exclaimed:

I'll heat up last night's soup—hmp there's some left over!

Mother appeared on the porch, and called across the lawn to Aunty Katie,

Kay, Charley's here with Eloise and the kids. Tell Mary to come in and make some sandwiches. They'll probably be hungry.

Aunty Katie's face darkened, and she said,

I *know* that. That's what I'm doing! Tell Charley we'll be in, in a minute!

Mother's face darkened too, and her eyes got a little chilly, and she said, well,

Well, he's *here*. That's where I got that from.

I snuck around the back of the house, went by the cistern and through the back door into my room, up two steps into and along the small back hallway passing the bathroom, turned left, went through the library and into the living room. I stood behind the glaze in the glass doors by the upright piano, and watched all my aunts and Mother embrace their brother, his wife, and three daughters plus a baby that could hardly see, in front of me, the words and sounds loaded with affection and kindness, and I frowned because it made no sense at all, so I smiled: sure it did. My eyes met hers.

Hi! Cuz Fee, called Cathy, big grin. Then she blushed.

I grinned. Cuz Fee. As I made the small return my heart jumped, seeing her well-ordered nervous reckless enthusiasm under dark brown bangs, and with her heavy eyebrows, and her dark flashing eyes right on mine she lowered them quickly, making still her red lips, in a glint of two big radish white teeth, as I trembled in my tracks. As the Uncle Charley tornado whirled by, missing me, and settled noisily in the living room. I faded around the doorjamb into the front hall where they had been standing, and as they moved into the living room, I said, with a half-fake smile and my eyes betraying me as I glanced at my magic cousin Cathy, in my curiosity,

Hi, Aunt Eloise.

In the shifting crowd she seemed to turn four ways at once, but then, recognizing me, made a slow zigzag smile and discovered herself, said hello, went into the living room with Serena in her arms, sat down nervously looking through her round steel-rimmed glasses out and around the room at everybody all talking at once except her three daughters, who sat with their knees together, their feet apart, and their hands in their laps: with hardly a glance at anyone, Aunt Eloise asked, in a shy voice, politely, with a caw:

Could ah have a cup of coffee?

Fee dear, Mother said royally, go out and help Mary, would you? Tell her to make coffee for all of us. Except.

Charley, smiled Aunty Katie.

Suddenly Aunty Mary ran into the living room wiping her hands on her apron saying coffee'll be ready in a minute and so hmp will the sandwiches. She sat down at the piano, and began to play and sing a song she had composed from one of Grandfather's poems, each line ending with the same three words, all (with a lift), pause, so (dipping) gaaayyy, and the last line ending like the others, but going up: all (lift), so (higher), (highest) gaaayyy!

Everyone generally patted their hands, and then Mother, Katie, Mildred, Dorothy, Charley, Eloise, and the kids erupted into talk and laughter as Aunty Mary rose, and laughing explained it all to us, about Papa's poetry, and how she had, etc., we all knew it, especially Papa, etc., through her, with a big smile that meant she saw herself before all of us, and in a confused flurry turned and went through the front hall into the dining room and then into the kitchen and began bouncing cups and saucers around, with silverware, on a painted tin tray.

I had been leaning on the kitchen doorjamb, and was about to go in to help, when I heard the front door open. I turned, and my sister came in, out of breath and brightly laughing—

I saw the truck! Uncle *Charley's* here!

We laughed.

I watched her. She went into the living room like somebody opening windows, and approached him saying Oh Uncle Charley, how *swell* to see you!

Then she burst into laughter because Uncle Charley, who had been yelling at Dorothy, hardly noticed, and then he did, and was brusque in his embrace, and kiss, and as she pulled up a chair beside him he began to shout about the prices, crops, the war, and bad luck. I went into the kitchen. Jesus.

Aunty Mary was making her usual gruesome peanut butter sandwiches. Slapped a blob of the oleo I had mixed onto a slice of white bread, slapped a blob of hard dry peanut butter in the center of another slice and clapped 'em together, singing, All so gaaayyy!

Aunty *Mary:* LET ME DO IT!

I can do it!

No, you CAN'T! I shouted.

Yes I can hmp, get coffee cups saucers napkins on the tray the water's boiling, the jay birds are back! Get the Postum for Charley!

Making peanut butter sandwiches was something I could really do. The ones she made would rip and tear, and she didn't care. They would know. I went tense in anger.

Please, Aunty Mary. Let me make them!

Blam! another one and she thrust me to one side saying No! MP No! Load the tray!

I did, and then I walked out of the kitchen, and went down the back hallway into my room, walked in a couple of circles and as everything seemed distorted or distracted, I went outside and down the back driveway which curved

around our nextdoor neighbor's house and out onto the
street, where I walked north to Matthews' Field, but nobody
was there.

I walked under apple trees to the barn at the east end of
the field, and watched the Matthews' farmer, Gus, at work,
following him around, which he was used to. He rarely said
anything to anybody, although he spoke to himself, under
his breath, he was an old man, big and stooped from
carrying pails of sweet milk all his life, and he wore the
same kind of farmer's overalls that Uncle Charley did, the
ones with the straps. I had worn them too, in Muddy Run,
in Pennsylvania. We all liked Gus, and in his way I guess Gus
liked us too, occasionally we helped him, get something for
him, you know, so he let us alone, he thought we were crazy,
and we never teased him 'cause he had a temper, he moved
fast when he wanted, and well there was a way the cows
looked at him. They knew, and cows can move fast when
they want to, too, but Gus wore a large sweat-stained floppy
hat, and though he was a patient old man, when a cow got
extra stubborn Gus's eyes got extra hard, and after he had
finally gotten the cow into the barn and the cow wouldn't go
in her stall, Gus's eyes kind of glowed out from under the
brim of his hat, and the two of them stood there in hay and
a little cowshit looking at each other, the cow getting that
look they have when they're making it a little tougher than
usual, an ornery straight-on look, and old Gus stood there
and looked right on back at her, her with her big brown
eyes, and he raised his hand and pointed into the stall, and
in his gruff quiet way ordered her in, and she didn't move.

"Go on," he said. "You know the way." Then he
chuckled to himself.

She swung her tail, lowered her head and pretended to
look around for something on the floor. Then went into the
stall.

He turned, and glanced at me, one eye from under a
shaggy eyebrow and I grinned and he nodded as I turned

and walked back outside. He didn't like anyone around when he milked. I went along the edge of the field and picked an apple, they were green, but I didn't mind, I ate one, and as there were several on the ground that were half rotten, I got a bunch and walked away from the tree, into the field, where I stopped, dropped the apples on the grass, and fixing the spot on the tree trunk where the second baseman's glove would be, I backed up a little, and then ran in, scooped up an apple, and fired to second for the out, and when I got tired of that I practiced my outfield throw, and partly worn out and partly in my fog-state, I ambled back to the barn. Gus was standing in the doorway lighting his dimestore corncob, puffing smoke, and I watched him. When he got it lit he pointed the stem at the apple in my hand and tossed away the match stick, shook his head a little, and said, Ye keep eatin' them green apples ye'll get the shits, and I began to laugh, I leaned against the barn holding my stomach I was laughing so hard, the cussword from him, and he shook his head, puffed on his pipe, turned and went back inside the barn. I heard him going up the steps into the hayloft.

I went home, and on the way I caught sight of the O in the STOP sign on the corner, I dropped the apple, and as it made a crooked bounce I yelled,

"The SHITS!"

recovered it, and threw with all my strength and missed. But I hit the sign. So, even so, he could have fielded it. For the out.

I walked home smelling the apple on my breath, and fingers, and in pure sensation I missed seeing Uncle Charley's truck make a U-turn, and head back the way he came, with the girls in the back waving to me and crying my name. Then I saw them, and waved back, guiltily and sadly, feeling a little lonely. I looked up at the sky as his truck got to the corner on the top of the hill, and after stopping for a moment, went on its way.

The sun was in its place, in the afternoon, and just to check up on myself, I figured I'd take a look at the sundial, even though I knew what it would say, but I loved the feeling of being right, so I did. I cut across the front yard and went around in back, where Aunty Mary had been in the rose patch, and passing the slab-concrete bench, I stood by the silent sundial, looking downward at the back-slanting triangle, set on the disc which was embedded into the top of the four-foot-high miniature Corinthian cement pillar. The triangle and the disc were beautifully mottled: green bronze, and the projected razor-edged shadow nested neatly there between the Roman numerals 4 and 5, which in spite of daylight savings the sun had already told me.

One afternoon I came home from school, and there was Uncle Charley's truck, parked on a tilt in its place by the bushes at the end of the front walk, and letting curiosity in, me and my fog went up the walk into the house where I saw him in the living room with my Aunt Dorothy (Dorf), talking loudly about crops, the prices, the war, and bad luck.

I saw my sister in a chair in the corner, half silhouetted against the front window, and for a second I thought it was Mother, smoking a cigarette. Uncle Charley's voice was tense.

I went in quietly, put my books on top of the piano, and sat down on the piano bench, and listened.

I KNOW, he shouted, AND GODDAMMIT I DO—

Charley—

WELL I *DO* KNOW, DOROTHY, AND I'M TELLING YOU IT'S BAD, I CAN'T SEEM TO DO ANYTHING RIGHT AND NOTHING SEEMS SET UP FOR ME TO *DO* RIGHT, D'YA UNDERSTAND?

We nodded.

He stood up and paced the floor in his faded work shirt, worn, dirty overalls, and heavy, thick-soled boots, face haggard and tired, but gaunt, angry, and wild. I watched as he reached into his pocket with one hand and pulled out a three-fingered clump of raw tobacco, and with the other hand a cigarette paper, and as he paced the floor he rolled a cigarette, dropping tobacco on the rug. Really Charley, Aunty Dot said, and then laughed, and so did my sister and so did I, as he said loudly that he wanted another cup of coffee and not Postum, and raising the cup from the table, finished it, and as he put it back in its saucer on the table, he staggered to his left, and regained himself, as Dorf said,

No, Charley. You know what it does to you!

He threw his hands in the air, and walked crazily around the room, shouting and grumbling, as she said,

Why don't you rest a while in Mouse and Fee's room —then she laughed.

He did too, and yelled,

DO YOU THINK A NAP IS WHAT I NEED?

Well, you're tired and upset.

A few minutes later, when I was in the kitchen drinking some milk, I heard Dorf say, here

Take this, dear.

His honest responding voice was hushed in humility. But strange, like at the theater. Thanks Dot, you've been wonderful.

Well, we love you and want to help.

I know you do. I love you too. It means a lot.

Goodbye, Charley, she murmured.

Goodbye, Dot. I'll call you next week. Love to the girls—

Yes, of course, and our love to Eloise and the children.

Soft sound of door opening and closing. I stood in the kitchen still hearing the distinct direct words. I didn't know they existed, like that. In our house.

My sister came into the kitchen, and seeing me, paused in the doorway. Our eyes met, and she said, grimly,

Boy, I love that man.

I nodded. Me too.

My sister's nickname was Ca, as in ka-*bam:* reality plus. But in full her name was the same as Mother's: Cara, except everybody called my sister Cara Junior, which she hated.

That was probably my romantic father's idea, so in love with his wife he named their only daughter after her. Mother, impressed but shy, agreed. Who could argue with love?

In those days.

In 1925.

In New York.

We'd all gone out to Uncle Charley's farm for a visit. Hillsboro, Missouri, a three-building, gasoline-station post-office grocery and feed-store town, the road went up the side of a hill so steep we only drove halfway, and then got out and walked the rest.

His farm was right on top. His crops were overgrown with weeds, and he couldn't get anybody to help him because he didn't have any money and even if he had, all the men were in the war. He had one man who helped, an old black man who stayed around because there was no place else to go.

My sister and me went for a walk.

We held hands and wandered through grass gone to seed. We ate grapes, picked blueberries and flowers, watched bees gather honey, and we chewed the stems of sweetgrass, and looked out along the wonderful view of the hills and valleys in the four directions under the blue midwestern sky, where an occasional puff of cloud drifted by.

She said, suddenly—Look. She knelt at the base of a post where grapes sagged on wild vines, and where the shaft entered the earth in sienna, she parted long ripe brilliant green blades of grass, and revealed violets, and I bent, then knelt beside her and we gazed into that tiny little shady corner of the universe letting our cheeks graze under our tender awe, words flowing on our breath *Gee whiz they're beautiful,* in perfume of earth, grapes, grass, and violets. She let the blades of grass return as they had been, and we rose and returned to Uncle Charley's farmhouse, with its broken furniture, bent utensils, and a despair that likened to that cracked and bare-knuckled poverty we had seen in

Pittsburgh, Florida, the mountains of Pennsylvania, and the places along the way to Missouri through the thirties where poor people stood in the dust with their empty hands, and drawn faces, by gas stations, bus depots, and post offices or by the sides of roads all across America in that soft and invisible, vehement slow-footed move to the horizon: The People. The poor. The people at which my sister and I stared, silently, sadly, in our journey to Kirkwood, Missouri, for a place to live, while our father tried to find a job in New York, and everybody stared at the horizon. Then. And in 1941 our father came home to die. And on top of a hill it turned into Uncle Charley's sagging and broken corncrib which fed only the rats, against the future placed in my memory not to ever leave.

I sat in the front seat of the car beside my Uncle Mouse, and when we had begun to drive home, leaving Hillsboro, he glanced at me, and said,

You're awful quiet today. What's the matter?

Turning in the seat so I could look at him, I asked,

Uncle Charley's really poor, isn't he?

Yeah, he said, as the car swung onto Highway 66. And Eloise and the kids think we're rich.

Shultz! Steve cried to Gary. Sig heil!

Sig heil, Shultz! we echoed, and at his puzzled expression—

Steve: *Shultz,* sig heil!

ACHTUNG! Gary yelled back—we jumped to attention.

The creek began on the other side of Taylor Avenue—in fact I thought it came from across the other side of Kirkwood Road—west of Kirkwood Road (beyond that I didn't know), and then moved its way down along the edge of Mr. Biggs's back yard to the front of his property where the creek went under Taylor through a concrete tunnel, and came out in Lizard's front yard, curved under the bridge which was a continuation of the driveway—the driveway that led to Gary's house, and then to Steve, Hobey, and Jan's house.

The creek then curved and marked the southernmost boundary of all of Gary's back yard, as it continued to do all the way downfield to the streetcar trestle which marked the lowermost southeast corner of Hobey, Steve, and Jan's big yard. The creek went under the trestle there, and continued east about four hundred yards roughly following the streetcar tracks until it disappeared under the distant bridge at Woodlawn Avenue.

Taylor and Woodlawn ran parallel, and were connected by Gil Avenue which extended into Orrick Lane like the cross bar of an H. Orrick Lane began almost exactly across the street (Taylor), from the end of my front walk. Except for Taylor, my front walk would have gone right into Orrick Lane.

But where the creek left Steve's property and went under the trestle was where we had not only an airport, but also small caves where we stored things. The creek bed was deep there, at least six feet to the bottom, and on overnights we pitched our tents or built our lean-tos on the top of the cliff by the edge, rather than dig big caves in the side (like we did in the old golf course), because the dirt cliff by the creek was too soft, and anyway our folks wouldn't let us.

At night we lay awake on blankets on top of the cliff by a little fire, and snuck a smoke, listening to the creek below, seeing the outline of the trestle low against the sky, and the stars.

During the day, with our toy trucks, ambulances, planes, and artillery, we made bunkers, underground bombshelters, and hangars. We set up our antiaircraft guns, and waited for the enemy, eyes peeled, passing the binoculars back and forth, waiting for Wimp with his Stuka to come around the corner of Steve's house, or low across the grass by the barn and then along the bushes by the creek.

The landing field was really neat because we could *dig,* tear out grass and build what we wanted.

That corner of Steve's yard was really big, and had tall grass, and long dry thin stalks with which we fenced, if we weren't smoking them, and we fenced fairly carefully because the ends were sharp, but tempers flared anyway, and I edged away, afraid.

When it rained the creek became a torrent, and after the worst rains it became a miniature Mississippi River with its slow swirling muddy whirlpools in the soft warm continuing drizzle the next day, and we stood around barefoot in swimsuits, watching, doomed and fascinated, as it wrecked our hangars, little caves, bunkers, bombshelters and not so gradually overflowed the bank, and sweeping across our airfield, covered the whole of that section of their yard, while we waded around complaining, and angry, in the enthusiastic understanding that we'd have to build the whole thing all over again.

We watched the brown water swirl along under the streetcar trestle in an utter dread fascination of what I, and the others too, had seen in the mile-wide Mississippi as it swirled so slow and relentlessly along under the great Eads Bridge in downtown St. Louis, except that was natural might in a force beyond us although I could feel it, so deep with such complicated currents, whirlpools, and a flat brown stillness with yellow in it that held me exact in suspense as I stood at the rail of the river boat, eating a hotdog, and looking down over the rail, watching the river, ever-moving along at the foot of high bluffs I dreamed about. Dreaming, will dream.

A line of trees and bushes, like a natural wall, separated Steve's property from the streetcar tracks which headed north, toward the old and abandoned golf course, and the field behind Matthews' Barn where the cows grazed, but there the streetcar tracks took a ninety-degree right turn, and headed east toward Woodlawn and St. Louis beyond.

I was mystified by the vision of the creek continuing through—under the trestle—and somehow running parallel to the streetcar tracks after their abrupt turn, as if the tracks had turned to go along with the creek.

Beyond the trees, trestle, and tracks was a field of high, grassy mounds and plains that stretched to Woodlawn. We called it The Lot.

It was to that lot and those mounds that we went, on breezy blue summer afternoons, to sled on folded cardboard boxes. A few of the mounds, and especially one —right beyond the trestle—were covered with long sweetgrass.

It was a beautiful little hill, about thirty feet high, and from a distance, as from Steve's house, we could see its grassy knoll over the tracks, through the trees: curved and almost level, and as we stood on top we could see clear across to Woodlawn, where the creek went under the bridge and disappeared into the woods, a little like the streetcar.

The bigger the boxes the better, and if we got a really big box, we got inside, and after a shove we slid and tumbled over and over and over until corners split. We held our flattened boxes before us like sleds, and we ran, bellyflopped, and swiftly slid smoothly to the bottom in a pungent grass smell, the fat blue summer sky above.

The ground was soft, and at bottom with the box beside me, I rolled over, panting and laughing, and lay on my back, arms out, gazing up at the sky, hearing the cries of the others. I scrambled up to get to the top, to do it again! Again! AGAIN! Upward I climbed, dragging my box with me, and down again I went, the grass and the earth so perfect, and sweet, flat and juicy against the earth: yellowgreen against dark umber and flinging boxes to one side, one by one we ran and slid down the hill on our bare chests, arms out front like a diver's, and at the risk of a little scrape (who cared), we came up at the bottom, chests a little flushed, and sticky from the grass juice, smelling of it, and dirt too, as the blades bent and shone in the sun, like we did, when sliding was best. The cardboard was shiny as if the undersides had been greased, and when we went down on those cardboard sheets we really *went,* and spilled off at the bottom as we struck the upcurve of the next small mound. It was like getting dizzy, which I loved, but it was better, because it had a racing thing whereas when I spun myself, I merely spun around and around and fell dizzy and laughing, stomach turning, but when we went sledding on the grass it meant going fast, going fast right into it, and there was nothing like going fast into it.

And to do it again!

When July and August took over the sky, Missouri turned into a solar blast, especially if there was no rain. The long grass in The Lot dried, became crisp, and if anybody even thought fire, it lit, and when it did, though the causes were unknown and the neighborhood kids, even us, were blamed, in fact invariably, maybe in a sort of subtle kind of way. But, in all the things we were, and were not, and that we did and that we did not, setting The Lot on fire wasn't our style, and mostly, which was easy to know and easier to say, we were too busy making blast furnaces, playing guns, or planes, and building each of the things we played with, so, when we got those looks from certain authorized adults, in a curious way we understood because in another curious way we could look at ourselves in the same way, because it was scary, dangerous, fun, and prrretty neat when those big fire engines showed up, and as we stood around watching the firemen glance at us, we saw ourselves in their eyes. They and other adults knew that it was flying burning paper from a back yard trashpit, or a tossed away lit cigarette.

But what irritated us was it was easier for them to give us dirty looks than it was for them to give adults those looks, or at least it seemed so, and anyway it wasn't fair, it didn't feel fair. It didn't take much imagination or many brains to know what one match would do, and it only took once to find out, and as the same neighbors had been living there for years, everybody knew when that lot got going, nothing could stop it. Especially if there was a good breeze.

Good breezes love dry grass and fire loves a wind.

The flames never got so high they damaged anything —houses, telephone poles or wires, or even trees, but it was a spectacle, and it gave the Kirkwood Fire Department something to do besides getting cats out of trees and making a mess of the back parking lot at Kroger's when the trash fire got out of hand. A grass fire was *something,* but of course when they got there their hoses weren't long enough so they tried to keep the fire within the range of their hoses, or vice versa, which was most likely coming at them so fiercely they had to get out of the way, and quick, too, which they liked and could talk about when they read their names in the paper next week, and anyway even if they didn't do anything, it gave them a chance to throw a little water around.

Anybody in the neighborhood who saw smoke called

the department and the kids and adults ran out to see and, if possible, to help. Especially us, which we sure did, and after the fire had burned most of The Lot, the firemen thanked us with their words doing tricks with their eyes, got on their big trucks and smoked back to the firehouse.

Steve's mom was standing in their yard, shielding her eyes from the sun with one hand, and gazing intently across the tracks.

"I see smoke," she said: we looked. Sure enough, a small plume of smoke wavered, and on a breeze, grew in strength and volume, and rose higher as it was blown toward Orrick Lane. Get the rakes and shovels, she told us, and I'll call the fire department.

We got the tools and met her on the grass, and cut across the yard to the gate, which wasn't a gate, but a wire on a post that went around a nail on another post, which we lifted and went through and onto the sharp bend in the streetcar tracks and then crossed onto The Lot, hearing a distant siren.

I looked down the line: not a streetcar in sight.

We walked toward the fire.

Steve's mom was lean with crystal gray eyes and short choppy brown and gray hair. She wore Levis, moccasins, and shirts that looked like men's shirts, tucked in flat under a beaded belt. I was generally afraid of her, and she knew it. She knew just about everything about me, and as we walked and ran up and down the mounds and through the tall dry scrub toward the smoke and flame, I had the sensation I was moving alongside a lithe, silent, fox-like, plain, and utterly beautiful creature. She made the best cinnamon toast I ever had, next to Mother's when I was sick, and she, Steve's mom, could handle an axe, a hammer, a rifle, or a car as well as any man, and as she was always tan, I had a further sense I was with a silky, paisley Indian woman, who was civilized over something savage that I hoped would never leave us. The firemen came across the field, waving and yelling, as she told us what to do, and went to tell them what that was.

Flames raced crackling.

Around a hundred yards ahead of it, in its path, we began to rake, and clear a swath as wide as possible, as neighbors and kids alike appeared and began to help, she returned.

Her body moved in a sweeping, intent rhythm, gray eyes glancing at the approaching blaze. The sky turned into a smoky graybrown filter.

We all coughed, to see what it would sound like, maybe the fire would hear us, or to test our voices to her, but neither was hearing, the fire was moving swiftly, and fiercely devouring the dry matted and tangled scrub and grass, crackling in a mad distant inhalation: smoke and fire came across distance in a low sustained whoosh about three feet high, smoke whirling and tossing upward in the breeze, changing the sky, but in no way did I fear.

Then, from just behind the dense smoke the fire was on us, it leaped across the brief swath we'd cleared, and as it was moving faster than we could run, when the tongues of it reached out to the other side of the swath we all jumped into and through it to sunshine and blue skies overhead, with no smell of smoke, save plenty of the smell of charred and smoldering grass. We stamped around and put the remains of the fire out so we could stand there together, and watch the fire go its way toward the tracks as the firemen chased it, tools in hand, swearing and gesturing and finally the hoses got going and we stood in warm ashes watching. I was impressed.

What I had loved was going through the flames.

She inspected our clothes and our legs, we were all okay, and as she knelt and looked at Hobey's, Steve's, and Jan's legs, and then at my legs which were like everybody else's, a little singed, she rubbed my legs and knees too, and then she glanced up into my eyes and we smiled.

She rose to her feet, and we went home, happy and chattering as the firemen stood in the far corner near the trestle talking about it too, while the fire burned itself out almost at their feet. They had doused the bushes on the other side of the tracks, though, which was good, and it had worked, so our airfield, though far away and not in danger, was safe.

Nancy Meyer wrote an editorial in the *Kirkwood* (weekly) *Messenger* which appeared the following week, about the danger of fire in our community.

It had started, the fire chief said, over by Woodlawn, and was probably caused (Woodlawn was a busy thoroughfare) by a cigarette thrown from a car, which meant that we were off the hook, because no kids lived anywhere near there. It must have been an adult.

She drove with the top down and right hand on the wheel, a Camel cigarette in her left hand, and her elbow on the window ledge. She took us out to Sugar Creek where we gathered leaves, ferns, flowers, stones, and watched birds, frogs, minnows, waterspiders, turtles, and walked and listened in those beautiful woods: in shadows sunny splashes of green and yellow, blue reflecting up from crystal pools, downward slanting through the treetops, we moved, holding our gifts.

What a beautiful smile she had.

Something, then, moved within me as I came alert in the autumn, in the chill Missouri October.

She'd chop wood, make a fire, and sit by the hearth gazing into the flames reflected in her eyes, and I sat by her as often as I could which was as often as I dared, which was not often, but occasionally, looking across the brief distance into her handsome flame-lit face and features, wondering what she was thinking, wondering what I was feeling if I dared to wonder that, which I didn't but secretly did, in love, baffled and in awe, and as I didn't stare, but glanced or secretly watched, fascinated, yet she never said stop it, nor did she ask that I not look at her, although after a while when it got dark she would say and often did, go on home Fee, which told me something simple I couldn't fathom, as I trudged my way home, the wood smoke of her still on me, in the dark on the leaf-strewn street as I wondered and wondered.

Steve, Hobey, and Jan's dad was called neither Pop nor Dad, but in the sound of it (to us too), we called him Pap, probably because it popped when we said it, with gusto, and snap: an executive, read magazines like *Fortune*, hated Roosevelt, and smoked Regent cigarettes. He was a neat man, tall, handsome, and cool, and generous, controlled his irritation when I showed up on Sundays before breakfast to see if anybody wanted to come out and play or maybe if I could come in and visit.

Their house was modern: one story, brick, with a gently sloping inverted V-shaped silver roof, casement windows, aluminum-trimmed glass doors that opened quietly onto the grass yard. No steps, no flagstones, but grass. The floor of the house was level with the yard: when you stepped outside you were in the yard. Even the adults agreed it was modern. The floor was cork.

This house was the center of neighborhood action.

While Hobey made his dazzling flying model airplanes and Jan took care of her horse Fire (whom she madly rode around and around the property, her long hair flying), and Steve painted landscapes, and their mother took care— literally—of the house, we came and went. I read the sports page and watched, and listened, and absorbed everyone and everything including their dog Jack, in an intensity that I could scarcely bring into speech, because the mystery of their modern *home*, as against my tired, old, historical Victorian house full of women, was too much to even dare to feel in the way I felt Steve's house and home, anxious and impatient I became, and went down the street, so Steve and Hobey were my brothers, Jan my sister and in the early 1940s when the bunch of us played with their large smooth hardwood blocks, actually building real pyramids, with secret corridors, or great fortresses with sliding doors as the rug became land and the hard cork floor the ocean, and the whole living room the world, I almost knew I was living vicariously.

Every birthday Steve had, he got as many silver dollars as his years, and like Hobey and Jan, each of them was also given something that they really wanted, and when Hobey turned fifteen Pap got him an English MG sportscar with wire spokes on the wheels, and a convertible top, but the hitch was the car wouldn't work, and Pap said if Hobey could fix it the car was his. But no matter how hard Hobey worked, as the weeks and months went by, it was no go, he couldn't fix it, so we took turns driving while the others pushed, fun downhill but uphill was a pain, yet worth it, from the top of the yard near the fence by the cows in the pasture behind Matthews' Barn, as we pushed the car downhill toward our airfield, the creek, and the trestle.

One night—like many—we roasted marshmallows over a fire in the yard near the pasture. It was when I was about to graduate from grade school (John Pitman), and had made new and future friends, and felt a change taking place that I wanted but feared, one night Pap invited all of us over and after it got dark and we'd had the marshmallows, and were sitting in a circle around the fire, he opened the book he was holding, and smiled to us saying he was going to read us a story he was sure we wouldn't forget, one he himself had never forgotten, as it was, he said, a favorite around the world. I glanced across at her as she sat with her chin on her forearms, arms around her raised knees, and staring into the fire, the firelight reflected in her gray eyes, as again really in her own gaze I saw the most dangerous game, he said, as we cheered Pap! Pap! and I felt a chill, I joined in, fantastically excited, Pap! each of us, hearts in our mouths, listened as he read, and it was a *terrific* story.

I asked Mother, angrily showing curiosity: Why can't you be like Steve and Hobey's mom?

I left my room to go into the kitchen to make a peanut butter sandwich, and saw Viola dusting Grandfather's bookcase in the hallway. She smiled hello as softly as always, and I grinned hi in return, asked how she was and she said she was fine, and how was I?

Okay, I said, and went into the kitchen, feeling the waves from her warmth on me: her small full brown figure, slender ankles, and dark eyes above a glint of gold on white front teeth. Dimples in her round brown cheeks.

Last year (1939) on her birthday, I gave her the small copy of the sphere and pylon of the New York World's Fair that I'd made out of clay, and when it hardened I painted it white, and as I gave it to her it broke in my hands and I almost wept, but in spite of me she took it, saying it was all right. It wasn't and I was miserable. I'd *really* worked on it.

Her husband Lawrence (who fixed it), was a foreman at the brick factory near Clayton, and he was built like a medium-sized brick. But darker than she. I thought he was awesome, and he didn't have to say a word to make me feel that way, though when he did my ears opened in a new way.

Schultz! Steve cried, and threw up his arm in the Nazi salute—to Gary: Ach *Himmel!*

Sig Heil! Shultz, we cried, Steve: Aw *Shultz.*

ACHTUNG! Gary yelled back, the heels of his sneakers making a soft thud as they came together—his right arm shot up. We jumped to attention as he laughed, he had a sharp, edgy laugh.

We milled around on the sidewalk on Kirkwood Road in front of Woolworth's, watching the little Philippine man carving South Sea scenes on one yo-yo after another that kids, after having bought them inside, brought them outside so he could make his designs. For a dime.

But we were waiting for John Hook.

Inside the dime store, on the left side in the second aisle, yo-yos lay in piles in their respective price ranges: nickel size, dime size, and two-bit size. The nickel size was small, about two inches in diameter and chubby, one side black and the other red, in a matte finish. The dime size was larger, glossier, and thinner. The two-bit size was tin, and had small holes, like portholes, along the edges of both sides, so when it got going it would sing.

Well, and the dime yo-yo was better than the nickel one, and the two-bit tin job was really neat, except that I liked wood and not metal, the singing didn't mean much to me, I could sing, and the Philippine man couldn't carve on tin for sure, so I gazed and gazed at the simple yet intricate scene he carved on my yo-yo, not so much because of the scene pictured, palm trees, and a sense of the horizon, though that too, but what I saw were his flickering fingers, and quick wrist-turns: how he did it.

For a nickel, or a dime, I could have all that, plus the important fact that on the wooden yo-yos the thing was to gently undo both sides, wax the wooden axle, and loop the string around, replace the sides, and walk around town throwing endless circles, as the string had no grip and the yo-yo spun at the farthest reach of the string without effort, or, on a straight down plumb line as I walked along it spun and slept at the end of its string. Also, at the risk of chipping it, and marring the scene of the South Seas, I let it walk, on the sidewalk beside me down Kirkwood Road.

John Hook came toward us.

He had a gait, he had a muscular build, a head like a box with a cowlick and a monkey face with a big mouth and white animal teeth and a wild twinkle in his big bug eyes and he could steal anything, which delighted me as I generally was the one who kept us supplied with comic books, candy, and cigarettes, stolen from not-too-careful Irish Catholic store owners—we were all Episcopal and John, who enjoyed stealing, and was especially fond of lifting yo-yos, was one of those Midwest church members maybe Baptist or something that nobody Protestant ever knew anything about except that they continually had good pitching in the church softball league.

On sight of John, rolling along toward us, we began to laugh, and when he joined us, we put our arms around each other and moved out of vision around from the large plate glass dime store windows back into the alley and made our plans. Hardly coherent. We talked about money.

John outlined the action we knew by heart anyway, but it was to hear him and watch him that was the thrill before the action, and in delight's envy, a certain overflow willingness: point in my character that caused me to overlook everything in my passion to do it right and then do it again just to make sure, yet, as John being John, the thrill to make my head spin, was to do one thing once so completely it included any following flourish, no reassurance with him and that was *John:* the neat flourish to begin with, because when John Hook showed up, he completed the action we had begun by waiting for him, because he could hook anything, his last name was not Hook and it was not me who named him, in my crystal laughter, and when I went in the dime store with my nickel in my hand, and made a purchase and so distracted the salesgirl, I became aware of the fleeting sunshine shadow behind me moving

down the aisle to my left selecting yo-yos as my breath
came fast in no way was I cool: my eyes were so bright I
feared, like in love they'd give me away, I mean there he
was right there, that Robert Louis Stevenson thief in the
aisle choosing the best as I completed my purchase and
in a signal whistle, I left, as the Hook shadow melted
outside onto the sidewalk.

Into the alley: John showed us what he'd hooked, and
our eyes lit up as he distributed merchandise, I fielded an
invisible grounder over second, made the pivot, stepped on
the bag and threw to first for the double play, we calmly
walked back out onto the street to the Philippine yo-yo
artist, who, with a few kids around him, surely caught our
aura, and folding and putting his knife in his pocket, in
answer to our requests, rose and did a few tricks with a
yo-yo that made us gape, the air stood still for his yo-yo
could sleep as if forever no matter where it went, and he
made it walk, sing, go around the world, he rocked the
cradle with an ease and skill that caused us and surely,
especially me, to not only be amazed at the yo-yo doing
those things, but to want to be the man who could make
them happen.

He sat, poker faced and intense in effort, slightly bent on
his little folding chair on the sidewalk in front of Woolworth's on Kirkwood Road, beside me, as traffic went its
way like adults: unnoticed, and I intently bent as he began
to carve on my nickel yo-yo, as my pals breathed down my
neck, watching his thin brown wrist and fingers skillfully
carving the trunk of the palm tree, then a coconut, the
palm leaves, and across the horizon in a sort of ripple he
carved my name. At once the water, a world toward
Mandalay in a vision of distant lands beyond, I saw the tiny
curlicues of wood as he blew them away, and the neat
flowing cuts in the wood, and my dilated eyes saw the wood
in my name and trees showing out from the matte paint,
and as he handed it to me and I gave him his dime he made

a curt nod, and in a glance raised his eyes to see who was next, as the kids pushed and shoved, and I , greed satiated in his transient's blank gaze, backed away and studied my prize. We all compared our yo-yos, and I, staring at my name, was the real thief, or if I could be, I would, to steal and be him, as we walked away, went down Argonne Drive, in a divided magic with John, to the bank of grass alongside the Missouri Pacific railroad tracks, where I took my yo-yo apart carefully, and fixed it so it could sleep.

Cuz Mary Lou visited and well they didn't know what to do with her big laugh at seven years old and there was discussion, so somebody said something and she was given a room to play in. So she found some crayons—it was in Aunty Mary's room where she was drawing on paper when Aunty Mary came in, aghast,

What are you doing!

Drawing with crayons, Mary Lou said.

But I didn't say you could mp, in my room.

Yes you did.

I did? (Searching)

And the ripples ran through the family as Mary Lou drew where or with what no one having told her, adults wondering, and then when I had the mumps I chased Mary Lou through the house, finger out, to touch my mumps to her as she screamed.

At John Pitman grade school, where we all went, the playground was asphalt, the cyclone fences were high, and, with a little luck once in a while, I'd find a nickel or a dime in the sand under the junglejim.

Hobey and the Lizard were in seventh grade at Nipher Junior High School, a mile away on South Kirkwood Road. Steve, Wimp, Cissie, and Jan were all younger than me, and though we met and played after school, in school I made new and different friends: Red Rodgers and Danny Hoffman, like Gene and Mac, were my closest friends. Red and I had a lot of fun spitting on each other.

At recess we raced around the playground: soccer, softball, volleyball, stopping to play marbles, flipcards, chew gum, eat candy, and talk and then play again, so wonderful, though the textured asphalt tore up our pants and knees, and elbows, as well as the balls we threw, kicked, and hit.

Recess was swell, but I didn't like school at all: I had too much Muddy Run in me: too many tiger lilies.

The woman who sold the grape, orange, and flavored milk drinks, and the cookies, had her little stand in the basement corridor, and on the cream-colored brick wall behind her was a real big framed photograph of General MacArthur, wearing his dark glasses, with his corncob pipe between his white lips.

Underneath the picture was his name and rank in the armed forces: the woman at the table beneath him had bobbed light gray hair, a pale, broad white face, rimless glasses, thin lips, and small cloudy eyes with black pupils that got hard when she got carried away about the greatest

American who ever lived, he'd return, and anybody that
didn't like Douglas MacArthur wasn't an American and
ought to be shot, which for some reason I took personally:
him too, because I couldn't see his eyes and why he smoked
that cheap pipe was beyond me, and through fifth and sixth
grades, as I got older, I mean, it was a tense moment to get a
cookie and some milk from her, as she sat beneath the
General and distant artillery as we marched further into the
war and I followed our boys on my big wall-sized map at
home, with different colored pins, in the Pacific and Europe.
My sister drew top secret maps for the U.S. Army Map
Service, which thrilled me, yet I remained confused by the
picture of General MacArthur and the angry woman who
sold cookies and soft drinks, and as I went into seventh
grade, and thus left John Pitman, they remained together in
Victory, and for a couple of years I had an odd memory of
MacArthur there, in cardboard under glass above the
cookie lady as she sold her sweet refreshments, and glared
out at me from beneath him.

In fifth grade, Mrs. Kelly read to us. She read *Black
Beauty*, and *Lassie*, and she wept so, especially at the end,
that she couldn't read, and she reminded me of the
engravings in the books my mother had read when she was
my age, of the woman in a tragic tale in a book called
Chatterbox, the woman's forehead resting on her arm as she
leaned against the mantlepiece, a hanky in one hand and a
letter in the other, and when Mrs. Kelly finished the story
we were all in tears too, and she closed the book tenderly,
looked at us and smiled, sniffling, and said,

There! Wasn't that *wonderful?*

And then.

Popeye.

I didn't—couldn't—really understand him but I wanted
to help him in my Christian way, yet the situations he
created were beyond either of us. He was everybody's
victim, and he got into so many fights his whole world was

fighting, but I never saw him start a fight and I never saw anybody take such beatings and fight back so fiercely. In fights without rules. He fought back in the kicking, biting free-for-alls that were always his to lose or fight to a draw, and we stood by and watched Popeye and at minimum two other boys fight to a deadlock so near true injury it was as if they were dogs, and in that odd fright, their bodies locked together, and then held, perhaps for protection, until the teachers ran out to angrily untangle them.

The big kids followed and taunted him, but I never saw him hurt anyone without their having asked for it. And in that sense he also fought with himself, as if he was somebody else to him, and he used to talk to himself like that.

Why! Why! he'd demand.

I dunno, he'd whisper back. I dunno.

He was in fourth grade, and sixteen years old: we were eleven and twelve in fifth and sixth grades. He couldn't go any farther. The teachers used the word retarded.

He was short and muscular and his large head tilted from side to side on his neck. His cleft jaw bulged out, his mouth was drawn back under his nose and his small eyes squinting were a little receded under his brow. One eye was set crooked. His light brown hair was thin, and generally low on one side, and he had a cowlick. He was short, narrow-waisted, and short-legged: he walked with his hands in fists, he dressed in worn tee shirts and worn pants, baggy socks and scuffed shoes. He was poor, and none of us knew where he lived, where he had come from, or anything about him except he appeared in school and on the playground. The teachers sternly told the boys to leave him alone, which the boys did until recess, or after school, when he came onto the playground, and they attacked him, in twos and threes, especially on rainy days when they were bored, and cruel in a premeditated adult way, taunting and following

88

and pestering him, as he shook his head and asked and asked and answered himself as the taunting got worse until suddenly he ran at, and then socked one boy, and turned and faced the other or others, but because he didn't have the strength he appeared to have—to knock them down so they stayed down—he could never win, for they always returned to taunt and follow him as he went wherever he went, alone to and in all of us, never winning but never losing those fights, bleeding just as they bled, he somehow survived to continue on his way, his solo fight against those kinds of boys who would be wherever he went, and as he liked me and I liked and admired him, gee he *always* came back, and he'd look at me, as we stood on the corner, he'd grin, wink a very sharp crooked eye, and laugh, punch my arm, and chuckle, then frown, shake his head, and glancing at me with a squint, cuss up a blue streak and demand, Why!

I dunno, we both answered.

Yet as he didn't come to school very often, or as often as we did, I only occasionally saw him, and he me. There was in my play a distance too complicated for me to cross, both in my fear of the boys who picked on him and the intensity of my playing, and too, his day-in and day-out world of violence wore me out, there was nothing I could do, I yet envied him, because he was constantly in a war, a personal war against a kind of boy I feared more than any other, and in fact that kind of boy was Popeye's element, and he stood out real. Although I could never cross over to him when at play, when I was at play—I mean no matter where I was or who I was with, in the shifting centers of softball or soccer action, if he waved and called my name, my heart leaped, and I responded with an outcry and a wave of my hand, too, but as I was where I was and that's what I was, playing, just as he was where he was in his way, I guess he knew better than me, that we were different. In his different way to know. But in the slow flat hours of grade school, in a despair of not being able to contemplate, and in my special fog where I was as if lost, even in the throng on the playground, trying to run and kick my ways in and out, I saw Popeye walking toward the street, head down, hands in fists, forlorn and alone. I saw him pass through a small circle of younger boys, and walk down the steps, I saw him as in a vision, in every sense outside us all, which hurt me, and yet as if beyond me, touched me over my head, and as the John Pitman days slowly became abstract weeks, one day I realized I hadn't seen Popeye in a while, so I asked around, but nobody knew, he often missed days at a stretch, but then suddenly it was a couple of months, so I asked the fourth grade teacher what had happened to Popeye, why isn't he in school? and she said, looking into my eyes which reminded me of Mother, sadly:

Popeye had to leave. That poor boy failed everything.

And in a day-to-day life I wouldn't let myself believe, I had lost someone, maybe in his way with himself, it was of me which I probably wouldn't ever find, to wave and call HIYA to, and to ask in a demand, Why! for the answer *I dunno* just as he did, or, in my way, to such an obvious and unfair cruelty, Why did Popeye leave? the answer because he failed everything, or, we don't know, I mean that truth of his failure in adult reasoning took the school out of John Pitman, and made it a building made out of bricks.

I walked home in the soft chill rain which that night turned into snow. I had my schoolbooks with me, and I crossed Washington and headed toward Taylor. I kicked through some wet leaves, and worried, I thought, about the soccer game, as I began a slow unwinding slide into fog, so that when I turned the corner, and headed down the street, the world faded and I fell deeper and deeper until I could hardly see the front yard I was walking across with no conscious sense or thought at all, and as I approached the front steps, I was almost out.

You're home, the voice said.

I looked up, and saw the front door, and heard voices within. I smelled Thanksgiving in seven and a half days. I smelled supper, too, and tasted rain on my lips. I went up the steps, and as I put my hand on the doorknob, the ice of brass snapped me into consciousness, and I had the sense I was trading places, and though I didn't know where I had just been I was sorry to have had to leave, I pulled the door open, and went inside my house in a feeling I'd just lost him something beautiful.

I fell in love with Norma in fourth grade. She had the longest pigtails of any girl, and her hair was very black. I sat behind her, and one day the tip of her pigtail fell right against the side of my inkwell. Hum. I never stopped loving her, she was so OH bee-yu-tee-ful!

Cecil Davis was the best ballplayer in fifth grade, and the fastest boy in grade school. He was thin, narrow-shouldered, narrow-waisted, and hollow-chested with a small arrowhead skull and kind soft blue eyes under a pile of soft blonde hair, generally shaved close on the sides. He was one of my favorite friends in the whole world.

He scored from first on Mac's long single to break the tie with the sixth grade, and with two out in the last inning my running catch gave us the game. Always the biggest game of the year for the fifth grade: the sixth graders took the loss hard, and we had to slow up on our teasing. My father sent me a thrilling mock front page tabloid headline from New York DAWSON CATCH SAVES GAME

FOR FIFTH GRADERS *Davis Scores Winning Run on Sloan Hit,* and the kids thought it was terrific. Especially Cecil.

He always looked hungry. He was poorer than most of us, and had a shy fragile quality that gave a leap to his speed on bases or in footraces, or in soccer when he got the ball: pass it to Cecil, he'll score, and when he did, he was breathless with it, and we shared the intensity in a brother feeling, though not as much with me as he and Red Rodgers did. He and Red were best friends. Red lived across a vacant lot from him, and when Red talked about Cecil his voice was soft and he looked in your eyes because Red was like that, and him and his folks knew that things were tough for Cecil at home, so as Red and I were friends I felt a mystery in Cecil being so close to Red—just across the lot from him—so when I visited Red, and we played, even if Cecil was with us, Cecil's house was always in the corner of my eye, over there.

My father sent me a ballglove that year, a great mitt, a Rawlings infielder's glove, and more than anyone at school, Cecil liked it, and when we were on different sides he always asked if he could use it and when I gave it to him his eyes shone as he put it on and smacked the pocket with his hand, running to position.

Your dad's really swell, he said.

He sure is, I said.

Cecil laughed, and moving before me backhanded an invisible grounder, threw to second for the force and caught the invisible return stepping on first for the double play as I pretended to play second.

Boy!

Then he was at first, and waiting for the real play.

The boys' diamond was near Washington Avenue, and the bases were painted. The girls' diamond was at the south end, alongside Adams, and across from the Presbyterian church. The smaller field for the little kids was west, alongside Kirkwood Road, and the basketball courts were there too.

I knew a boy named Gale West.

I knew a girl named Bobbie Vermillion.

The huge tree with the stone wall around its base, on top of which we sat, and ate lunch, and I stole food from Red, daily, just about, was where we played flipcards.

The hit bounced into right center, and as I went around first, Jim Righthouse, who was playing first, tripped me, and I fell, and went down hard on my teeth, and when they picked me up the tips of my two front teeth were gone. Jim was almost in tears he was so sorry, and he apologized and later we went down to Kirkwood and he bought me sodas and ice cream and a pile of comic books which we read together as he was apologizing and wondering why he did it. I shrugged my shoulders, and turned the page.

But at home later, after school, Mother was heartbroken Oh your *wonderful* teeth! Fee! What will we—Does it hurt? (No) Are you *sure?* Yeah, I'm okay. Well it's terrible. Poor Jim, he must feel awful. There were tears in her eyes as she inspected my teeth.

I nodded, and said Jim felt so bad we went down to Kirkwood, and—she mussed my hair and laughed as I told her. Look! I said, and showed her the comics. I know, she nodded, murmuring, Oh your lovely teeth, what will we do? Well, it could have been much worse, you won't need stitches in your lip, and everybody agreed I was lucky, and when we could get the money together I'd go to Doctor Mack and get them capped. I heard my Aunty Dot say, in the next room, Well kids are awful, just *awful,* so cruel to each other! Poor Fee, and Uncle Mouse said Yeah, for once he kept his mouth open.

I laughed. Secretly I didn't mind, because the attention

was real, and there was a lot of it. A little disfiguration didn't bother me.

I was shaken, though: I'd been physically hurt beyond my control, which surprised me, and I thought So, it can happen to me, and I understood a little better, what my body could take. Like Popeye.

Thursday evening

I was glad to get your letter telling how you broke your teeth. I could understand exactly how it happened. I'm glad you weren't hurt more badly. Mother told me a few days ago that you bit a piece of toast to show her it didn't hurt, so I guess you are practically well—and I'm glad of that. I hope Mother takes you to a dentist to have them fixed pretty soon. If the boy hadn't tripped you, do you think you would have made second base safely? I've been wondering about that.

When a fellow plays so hard, he's just bound to get hurt once in a while it seems. When my brother Guy was a little fellow, he was pitching horse-shoes, and another fellow just for fun was pretending to bat them with an axe as they sailed past him. Well, when Guy threw one the other fellow ran forward a few steps, and swung his axe and hit Guy right in the mouth with the back of the axe, and boy, did his mouth bleed. But he got over it and doesn't even have a scar.

Once when I was a little fellow, I was playing catch with another boy and he wanted me to throw the ball just as high as I could so he could catch it, so I did, just as high as I could, and he held up his hands to catch it, but as he saw it coming down, he got scared and pulled his hands down, and bent over almost double, way down low, and the ball came down and hit him right in the middle of the back, and he went home crying.

Well, I hope that you don't get hurt any more. Are you playing ball better than you used to? Can you catch better?

Lots of love to Mother and Cara and you and everyone else.

Dad

In the early spring of 1941, he came home sick. He was going to Barnes Hospital for an operation, soon, but meanwhile stayed in Mother's room, in her bed, and I visited him every day after school, and we exchanged the news. He had difficulty sitting up, but he was cheerful, although his face was pale because of the constant headaches. He knew lots of games, and once he asked me if I could draw an Indian and I said no, so he drew one, but he had difficulty holding the pencil, I wanted to help him, but he was frustrated and angry and wouldn't let me, it was all right, he said, we'll wait until another day when I'll show you, and he lay back in bed. Mother came in and gave me a look, so I left as she went to him. He had a way of drawing an Indian so that it made a word or something, like Uncle Mouse could sign his name Essex and make it look like a mouse, which he did on that postcard he sent me from the Lake of the Ozarks, saying he was surprised to see me there, he thought I was still in Kirkwood, and then signed his name Essex, but it looked like a mouse, and I turned the card over and there was a picture of a mule.

Before Daddy came home sick, he only visited on the big holidays and on his two-week vacations, but it was always wonderful. Steve and Hobey, and the Wimp and Lizard and all the kids came over and met him, and as they were half

95

crazy over Mouse, they were I thought startled that I had a father, too, so with Mouse, my dad and all the kids there, our house really came alive. Daddy and I built a plane together: a P-41 Flying Tiger. We worked hard on it, and afterwards put on the insignias and best of all the menacing Tiger's jaws, just behind the prop, and then the little numbers and things that made it real. We set it on the right-hand corner of Mouse's desk, and then, so it wouldn't be in Mouse's way, we hung it on a string from the ceiling on a slant as if it was diving, bright and shining: all ready for action.

Do you still have the fighter plane? he asked.

Sure, I said, looking at his head. It was swollen on the right temple.

Swell. How's school?

Okay, I lied. My friend Cecil loves the mitt you sent me, and I let him use it. He's poor, and lives across the lot from Red.

Good for you. How are your other friends, the girl with the horse—

They're okay, I said, but the horse has a cold.

He laughed, and asked what the horse's name was and I said Fire.

He chuckled, and then laughed again. He loved to laugh. Fire, he said, with a cold. But it's a nice name, for a girl's horse, and he asked me if I ever rode it, and I said no, it had a bad temper, a mean one, and he asked me if I was afraid of horses and I confessed I was, a little, although I had ridden at camp. He said he used to ride a lot, and loved it, and then he asked me how my fielding was coming, was I catching flies any better? Well, I said, shifting my feet, I'm practicing for the new season, and he said good, keep it up, and I nodded that I would and he said that was why he had sent me the glove, and I said, it is?

He nodded, amused. He said, "To catch flies with."

Then he clenched his fist, and closed his eyes. His face went pale. Something came in and clogged my throat and I had trouble breathing. Mother appeared with her hand on my shoulder softly saying I should run outside and play, Daddy was tired. He opened his eyes, and nodding, agreed with her, and then he winked.

I lowered my eyes and then raised them.

Come again, as soon as you can, he said, and closed his eyes. We shook hands and I backed away from the bed saying I would, not quite knowing where to look, in the spare white and green room, so I went to the next bed and said so long to the detective, who was sitting up halfway, but looking at the ceiling. He had tubes coming out of him, they said there was something wrong with his liver, and he smiled to me and said come again and I said I would. I returned to Daddy as Mother kissed him and fixed the sheets and stuff, and we left the room together, went into and along the corridor and then into the elevator and down in that smell, got off the elevator and went through the lobby out the front doors and down the steps and boy was I glad to get out of that hospital, and how I wanted to be back in that room with him, as we went to the parking lot to Uncle Mouse's Chevy coupe.

My sister and her best friend Louise Fox were sitting at the kitchen table drinking coffee and smoking cigarettes, talking in low tones, when I came in. She looked at me and asked how Daddy was. Okay, I said, but tired when Mother and I left.

She nodded.

Hi, Louise, I said.

Hi, Fee.

They began talking again and I went to my room, which I shared with Mouse, his room, actually, and he was at his desk putting stamps in small cellophane envelopes. I glanced at my fighter plane and crossed over to it, and looked up at it as it dove at my face. Something was in my throat, and I fiddled with the prop.

Hi Mouse, I said.

Hiya Feelin', he said quietly. How's Clarence?

Okay, I said. A little tired when we left. His head sure is swollen, though. That's where the tumor is, isn't it?

After the first operation Daddy was asleep in a lifeless way. His head was to one side, and he was breathing, and that was about all. We looked at him. My sister and I held hands. He was almost covered by sheets. I saw his left jaw, cheek, nostril, eye and ear and the rest was covered with bandages or under the sheet, head deep in pillows: I went to the next bed to say hello to the detective, but he was asleep too, breathing and with him that was about all too, not looking much like a detective to me, so feeling dizzy I looked around at the other patients, and then I went back and stood beside Mother and my sister. Daddy was so drugged it was like he was dead. The doctor (Cady) said the operation had been successful, Mother told us, but. Blank.

When we went back a couple of days later, he was sitting up. The right side of his head was flat, and bandaged. We talked a little, the nurse cranked the bed up so he could see us better, and after a while my sister Ca and I went into the noisy hospital coffee shop and had something to eat while Mother stayed. When we went back up she was putting on her coat, and I shook hands with him saying we'd see each other soon. He smiled with the right side of his mouth, the left side was frozen, and his eyes almost closed, they'd given him another injection, and I experienced a sense of something white and rancid in my throat and nasal passages not going away, glue slick. His face was very pale, as if totally exhausted. As we left I saw Mother was tightlipped and staring. I knew the word that seeped into and filled the room, and the hospital, and that hovered like an inner organ as we left the city and returned to Kirkwood, because I'd done some reading, and when Dr. Cady told Mother, I knew what malignant meant, also what it tasted like: gray rotten throat.

Which came in like fog. Dr. Cady operated once more, and it didn't work, nor did the treatment. Daddy was transferred to the (V.A.) Jefferson Barracks Hospital across the river, where they operated only to ease the pain. He lasted for several months, and we visited him often. I read about surgery, and studied tissue with my microscope (studied my spit, snot, and sperm, too). I studied blood slides, and planned and sketched operations, and read and reread *Microbe Hunters*. I was in the sixth grade. He lasted through the winter, and in April of the following year, 1942, he died. Mother told us that just before, the moment before he died, he came out of the coma, looked up at her, his face radiant—

"I see birds!" he cried.

She had moved close to him and had taken his hand.

"I see birds!" he exclaimed, cheerfully—"rising from rooftops!"

The morning of the funeral was beautiful and mysterious. April, and it had just rained. The trees, bushes, blades of grass, and flowers held crystal droplets, and the smell, the clean fresh smell on that clear April breeze and force of changing seasons held me in an ascending suspense, as birds sang and chirped, and flew among the soft sweet breezes of spring, crossing the damp earth where his body went. Everyone wept, not me, my sister stood close, we held hands as she wept too, and the minister read the service. I looked at the grave, and then at the trees. Clouds swept overhead.

September of the year before.

We sat on the top of the low rock concrete wall, and leaned against the cyclone fence which was embedded in it. Cecil asked me how my father was and I said not so good, and he asked what was wrong. He knew Daddy had come home from New York, and was in the V.A. hospital. I said my father had a brain tumor, and had had three operations in Barnes Hospital and Doctor Cady, the surgeon, had told Mother the tumor was malignant, they couldn't stop the growth, so when they cut it out, it would grow back again, feeling troubled to say it like that, but then, Mother had told us what Doctor Cady had told her, and it had been true: at first there had been some hope.

Cecil asked me where we had lived before we came to Kirkwood. Pennsylvania, I answered, and gripped my mitt, Cecil watching me. Our hands were dirty and we smelled slightly sour. I fingered the flipcards in my back pocket, visualizing the terrifying one of Japanese soldiers throwing gasoline on Chinese women and children, and setting fire to them in orange, yellow, brown, and blue, as he asked me where in Pennsylvania, and I told him about the summer in Muddy Run, and *tiger lilies* and in the telling I got too excited, and was panting, and recess was over and as we went back inside I wanted to tell him more about it, about Jess and the truck, and how I gathered apples and lay on my back in long grass and watched the sailing spiders. I felt anxious and angry and had difficulty breathing, it had been so wonderful, and I was tense and couldn't concentrate for the rest of the day, except on being funny, and from the teacher's point of view, a disturbance. After school I asked Cecil if I could walk him home, and he said swell, and as we walked up Kirkwood Road together I was so confused I couldn't talk, and we looked into store windows, and at the strange photographs of people being married that Francis Scheidigger had taken, displayed there in the window, the examples of his art. As we passed Chippewa Drugs I wanted an ice cream cone so bad I almost fainted, they had the best cones *anywhere* but I only had a couple of pennies so we got some bubble gum and laughed at the faces in the cartoon of a man kicking a cat, and a cartoon car that couldn't go in primary colors, and a few minutes later, near his house, we said so long, see ya at school tomorrow, and I watched him walk across the lot to his house which kept me out. I turned, and headed home, scuffing my shoes to feel the tips of my toes tingle, while blowing big pink Fleer's bubbles and flipping a few cards on the sidewalk. I lit up a smoke.

Boy!

I stopped, and listening, looked around. Beneath my feet the Missouri Pacific railroad tracks stretched in silver around the bend: east to St. Louis, and as I turned to see, west to Kansas City. I was standing in the middle of Kirkwood, Missouri, hearing the sound of distance in the echo of my father's voice, saying my name. He called me Boy, like in Tarzan, and again I was in his arms as we wrestled, in our house on Lehigh Street, in Pittsburgh—in the sun room where my sister and I built a tower of blocks as big as the Empire State Building and standing on chairs we made it as big as him, and he WORKED there! How he laughed! He *loved* to laugh, and *sing!* Oh boy, he *really* loved it, and Aunty Mary really LOVED *HIM!* and as I stood on the railroad tracks in the middle of Kirkwood and maybe of my whole country too, I looked across at the Episcopal church, on the small hill, steeple and cross against the late afternoon clouds, knowing how in the long

long swing to Mandalay everyone loved him. And, he sure loved *me*.

The day on Lehigh Street in Pittsburgh that we flew the kite! We spent almost all day together, and what a beautiful day! Run with it! he cried, run against the wind Boy! and he ran at my side holding the string just a little so I could hold it, I was seven—Give it play! and he gently tugged, and the kite lifted, I gave it play and the kite rose, dropped, he and I ran and then slowed, he and I carefully pulling the string taut, and then he jiggled it, and I imitated him, and the kite rose, up to the trees, and then over rooftops, and held, trembling, until a gust of wind took it as high as it could go, and with our kite in the sky we were out almost until supper, standing in front of Arthur's house, who was my friend. He had the best collection of Big Little Books there was, and especially on rainy afternoons I went over to Arthur's house and read his Big Little Books, we often swapped, for I had a good collection too. I made myself remember that when we next went to the hospital to see Daddy I'd ask him when we could fly our kite again, and I crossed the tracks and went home feeling like Pittsburgh, with him I didn't want to go to any hospital, to see him.

Mommy! When we go to the hospital again I'm going to ask Daddy when we when he and I, I'm gonna ask him when he gets well can he can we fly kites together—

KAZAN: Huskie of the North

Oh I grabbed him O K and *HUNG* on to: the thieving trapper in the Northern Canadian Wilds: I, Kazan: Huskie of the North, as I had waited and then come fast across the snow, leaped, and caught his leg between my jaws—we wrestled, I: determined, *never* let go! He fell! I had him! He yelled, seized me, tried to throw me off him, oh how he fought! but I *had* him—in the snow: pinned, *down!*

Panting, although he had been tough, and had nearly escaped me, I crouched over his fallen body, waiting for the Mounties, and he said, trapped at last, not daring to attempt escape, face up to my fangs, and my blazing fierce-dog eyes: he admitted:

"All right, Kazan, you've got me."

He stood up, lifting me with him, we laughed and embraced, he messed my hair, after the game of games, his game—*my* game of games   MOMMY I GOT HIM AGAIN grr, I warned him.

In his room in the hospital, his bed was the first one on the left as we went in, and he was sitting up, holding something to his ear, and was so involved he didn't see us, and as Mother reached his side, he looked up, saw her, and me and my sister, and made a sign for us not to speak, and for a moment we stood watching him.

He's listening to the radio, Mother said. It's a hospital radio. There's an earphone by every bed.

I nodded, as his face and eyes brightened, and with a difficult smile he lowered the ear-piece, clicked off the button, and said,

Creepy Crespi, the Cards' shortstop, just went behind second, caught a grounder, did a somersault in shallow right field, and while upside down threw the runner out at first.

We were astonished, but his laugh was a helpless grimace. The tumor in his right temple, that side of his head shaved bald, and the scars and stitches from the repeated operations showed red and blue against his dead-looking skin. They had unhinged the skin-flap and sliced off the malignant growth (I was determined Mother tell me the details), which, before they operated, made his head swell horribly on that side, but afterwards it was worse in a different way, his temple was flat again, but sunken and ugly, freshly stitched, and he was, then, as Mother said, absolutely exhausted, and a word I also knew—depressed. The left side of his face and body were completely paralyzed, and in visit after visit I saw what Mother and the adults understood better than I, that he had gradually lost his senses, and in a darkness of my own, the mind and body I'd flung myself against, as well as run alongside and so often embraced, went into coma and away, and when Danny Hoffman, Red, Steve and the kids, and Cecil, looked at me and said they were sorry my dad was so sick (their folks had told them), I knew, and thanked them while I clowned, but I wanted to *play*, I didn't want to be seen like him, who would? Let's play ball, or guns, or planes! I played marbles, flipcards, and Red and I spat on each other and chased ourselves around the playground screaming, and that miracle of a sixth grade teacher passed me, although I had failed everything except art, because, as she told Mother, Fielding has to get out of grade school, and into junior high, period.

In the fourth and fifth grades I had begun to draw pictures of Mother, and of animals, planes, and ships, and in the sixth grade I began the charcoal sketch of Pasteur, who was my hero as *Microbe Hunters* was The Book, especially the part about Pasteur, so I really worked hard on my portrait of him. It was big, about 12 × 18 inches, and I got so involved in it, it was about all I did, I very nearly didn't get to junior high because of it, and the disturbance I created (clowning), but I never stopped working on the drawing and I mean I worked right through the charcoal paper, used up a box of charcoal sticks and even a stick of pastel black, so in the end it was a complete mess.

But while I worked the other kids watched, and kept track of my progress, while I got one eye right and ruined the other, and had difficulty drawing his beard. Cecil watched me too, and showed enthusiasm not so much at what I was doing, but that I was doing it, and he made open and encouraging responses: how swell it was, that somebody could do that. Are you going to be an artist? he asked. If I can't be a doctor, I said.

We all graduated from grade school, and went across town to Nipher Junior High and the seventh grade. I made great promises of settling down to some serious work, no more clowning, and I told my friend Jack, who lived with his beautiful sister on Hollywood Lane, that I was through with goofing off, but as I had passed sixth grade by the skin of my already skinned teeth, paying attention to bright new textbooks in big new seventh grade with all those new teachers was just an advanced version of the same old crap, and I began my old clown-tricks again, and my recently acquired stammer got worse, with the five vowels sticking in my throat to nearly suffocate me, especially I, and my personality began a curious change—on guard! as I chose only words that began with consonants.

In eighth grade, while I was constantly drawing and painting, I was beginning to write stories and poems, and in the spring, just after I'd learned how to walk again after having been hit by the streetcar, in 1944, when I was staying up late reading or listening to the radio, and skipping school, I flunked math, biology, history, but not, but almost, English, and suddenly, realizing I hadn't seen him around, I asked Red, and he said Cecil had dropped out of school. *Cecil* dropped out?

"Your dad's really swell," he had said.
"Are you going to be an artist?"
Cecil's mother had committed suicide at the end of that

winter. One of his two brothers, both older, had left home, and as Cecil's father was an alcoholic, they were having difficulty getting Welfare, and Cecil had to quit school and get a job.

I want to kiss Norma!

It was late June, school was out, and I was standing by the sundial in the side yard, thinking in my fog that maybe I would go and see if the Lizard and Steve and Hobey wanted to play some ball, when Mother called me to where she was standing, on the step to the side porch, by the morning glories. It was a bright, hot afternoon.

Fee, she said, You've got to try and help me. You know how hard I try, and when you fail in school it makes things so much more difficult for all of us, and extra tough for me, because, dear, I'm going through a change in my life. Please, do your best, please, for me.

I sank. And down and down I went, in around and under and down and down and down in the ground.

"I will," I lied.

I went into the kitchen of my pal Gene's house. His mom was at the sink, cleaning carrots. I stood beside her.

"May I have a glass of water, Mrs. Reid?"

Sure thing! she said, warmly, in her soft southern accent. She drew me a glass of cool water, handed it down to me, and as I took it our eyes met, and as I drank, I looked up at her, never taking my eyes off hers as she gazed down at me, as I was realizing how beautiful she was, and after I finished drinking, I gave her the empty glass, which she put in the sink, and for a while I I stood beside her, going to her: so *warm,* she was.

Goddamn you, Ca said furiously, Can't you do better in school? You *know* Mother's upset. Can't you even *pass?*

She stood before me, her hands on her hips, near tears, in fury.

I lowered my head in shame, and—mumbled I'd try.

She was sitting Indian-style on the floor in her and
Mother's room, intently wrapping presents for my birthday
which was next week. I stood in the hall, looking in through
the doorway, watching her. She didn't know I was there. I
was in a fog again, but beyond myself, and I felt cruel.
Contemptuous of what she was doing.

I went into the room quietly, glanced at an unwrapped
present and sat on their big bed, folding my arms across my
chest and looking down at her, who, suddenly seeing me, in
alarm quickly with one hand hid the book behind her back,
and put the other over the box of different colored pastels
on the floor. She looked at me, helplessly confused, and
hurt, and cried angrily,

You *know* these are for you—

I made a flagrant gesture, and stammered, I don't—

Who wants I growled—I don't want to read that shit.
Twenty Thousand Leagues Un-under the Sea, who wants
to read that?

Her lips pressed together. Her eyebrows went up in hurt,
and her eyes narrowed in rage,

You ungrateful little son of a bitch— YOU'RE
GETTING THEM WHETHER YOU WANT THEM
OR NOT!

She burst into tears, put her face in her hands, and her
seated body shook as I left the room, head spinning, I
dizzily made my way downstairs, out the front door, around
the porch and into the side yard by the flowers. I went into
the little grass inlet and sat on the small cement bench near
the sundial, and then I rose and went to the sundial, and
looked down at it, and unseeingly read what the sun told

the shadow to say. Then I curled up on the grass, at the base, almost unable to breathe. I looked intently at the blades of grass, the tiny earth-globules at the base of each blade that the ants had rolled and gathered up there, and I watched an occasional ant scurry along. I gradually faded out, though after a while I rose, and going back around the back way and down the driveway I walked up Taylor to Bodley, and along Bodley to the huge deserted gray woodframe Gratz mansion, cut through the empty but vast, twig-scattered and gone-to-seed yard. I picked up a withered apple, threw it at a tree and missed, and crossed on over onto the deserted golf course, and making my way through tall grass and up hills and down into the little valleys, I came to the cave that Steve, the Lizard, Wimp, and Hobey and Jan and Cissie had made, and I went in, sat down in earth smell, and lit a candle.

I didn't go home until it was not quite dark, and sitting in the cave, I heard voices. At supper. Aunty Mary:

Where's Fee? I've looked everywhere, hmp.

He's prob'ly playin'. Aunty Mil.

His dinner'll get cold! He'll lose the vitamins! Aunty Dot (Dorf).

Knows better! Aunty Katie.

Vitamins don't know nuthin', murmured Mouse.

Mother laughed, and said, is my love a vitamin? and everybody laughed. Aunty Mary turned up her hearing aid, WHAT?

MARY, Katie said angrily, Turn it up BEFORE supper!

Mother yelled ESSEX SAYS FEE IS A VITAMIN MEANING HE DOESN'T NEED ANY VITAMINS! and everybody laughed again. Aunty Mary laughed too, scooped up a spoonful of soup with a hand so shaky it looked like somebody was shaking her, and she said, to the soup, with a frown,

Fee a vitamin hmp ha ha, guess so.
Let him starve, my sister thought.

I saw her the next day when I came home from school.
She was in the front yard doing a watercolor of the house,
and in shame and guilt I went to her side. She looked up and
smiled, but her lips quivered—I'd avoided her last night,
and felt pretty ashamed of myself.

I put my arm around her, and knelt beside her. She said,
"Want to see what I've done?"

"Sure!"

She opened the large watercolor pad, and I stammered
I wanted the book and was sorry about yesterday.

So am I, she said angrily, and as she held a picture up, I
looked at it.

Oh *gosh* in truth and sudden longing, "That's
wonderful!"

"Do you really think so?" she asked.

I nodded. She frowned and sighed, but showed me
the rest of the work in the book, and we talked about it. She
was so good there wasn't much I could say, and I wanted to
stay and watch her paint, and under the circumstances she
wanted me to, but I knew it would be better if I left, I could
see she was concentrating on it, so I kissed her on the cheek
and said so long, crossed the yard, and went up the steps
into the house. Before I went in, though, I looked back, and
she was at work again.

She was an acclaimed prize-winning water-colorist, and
also a poet, and in statewide contests ran either first or
second to her best friend, Louise, who to me was a really
terrific person. They were the same age—both five years
older than me, and had just graduated from high school.

I had stood, for a moment, watching my sister. Her right

hand moved deftly, her eyes were direct on the paper, and with a flair caught the spirit that the brushstroke in watercolor demanded, all her own, as our house appeared bright and clear, and a little wooden-looking which it was and I always felt and knew she liked to catch that.

I went into my room to get my glove and my DiMaggio bat, it never occurred to me, ever, that she might want, and had wanted, a room of her own, in that Victorian household established by loving, preoccupied middle-aged virgin women.

This was when she had the highly skilled job of drawing the ponds, creeks, bridges, hamlets, telephone poles, hillocks, hills, and valleys of Formosa, which the Army reconnaissance pilots had photographed, as the next scheduled target before the invasion of the Japanese mainland, if that invasion of Formosa were necessary, maps of which nobody knew about but me, because I had driven her three-quarters goofy begging to see even a little piece of what she was doing, and finally she showed me that little piece, making me PROMISE NOT to tell ANYBODY and I promised I wouldn't. I had a top secret, and I kept my word. Until the war was over.

After the streetcar accident.

The best ear specialists in the Midwest said I would soon be deaf in both ears so when I could walk I began to go into St. Louis, to the Institute for the Deaf, to take tests, and later when I was back in school, glad to be on my feet again, I still continued to go to that institute, because they wanted to check what was happening and see what progress my inevitable complete deafness was making.

I took lots of tests, including the spooky one which we had had in Pitman, and in junior high anyway, the one where the woman's voice vanishes, like on the other end of the string, tin can against her lips well it sounded tinny and the doctors said it wouldn't be long so I'd better prepare for the worst. So Mother broke the news about lip-reading lessons, even though I could hear perfectly with my left ear, thus included in my school program was my (tutored) training in reading lips, which meant I had to squeeze that in with the rest of my schedule, so they got me out of study hall, and that was great because I could sneak a smoke on the way, and on the way back, which Mrs. Parham, the study hall teacher, knew. She got a certain look when she knew we were doing anything shady, pursed her lips, got a sarcastic look, a sleepy look, in her eyes yeah, she was pretty tough, and sexy, talked easily, and she gave me the eye as I rose and began to tell her I was going to my lip-reading lesson—

Well Guy, then you best go, right?

Guy was my Christian name.

Right, I grinned.

I liked her. She was moody, though, but she was faithful to her mood, and she sure could show her anger. And she talked back to anybody. She watched us, and often there was a way that she sighed which was, or could be, her announcement that she was about to tease us. She'd look at me, sigh, make a little smile, and say, in her soft tough deep Missouri voice,

I don't know about you, Guy, but I have the feeling you might amount to something if only I could figure out what.

The kids laughed in that part of the room, along with me and Mrs. Parham.

She had a nifty way of teasing football players, and making bullies blush, which of course made a lot of us happy, and not necessarily just me. As I rose to leave, she moved across to me and said,

"Guy?"

I turned, books in hand, and looked at her.

Her complexion reminded me of Mr. Wiggins, and so did her hair. Her skin, like his, was a deep dusky color, and their hair was wiry. She wore her hair pulled back in a bun, it was very black, and so were her eyes. Her lips were thin, and she had a kind of Spanish look. Mr. Wiggins's face was broad, his lips were thick, sort of, and his nose was wide. His hair was black but graying, and short and in wiry little waves. He was a big man with broad stooped shoulders, a sense of right and wrong and a temper to match: a geometry teacher and the track coach, which he was with a passion. My sister had been one of his favorite students and he scared hell out of me because I didn't do as well as her. There was a way Mrs. Parham reminded me of him, which was probably her variation of his temper.

She looked at me, and as she looked her eyes widened and focused on nothing but the centers of my eyes, until her eyes were really Big, and she didn't say anything. She looked like a sore toad, made a curt nod, and turned away.

That was to let me know if I got caught smoking in the boys' room it would be pretty tough.

And too bad. Kid stuff got what it deserved, so to speak,

and having gotten the message, I left, walked down the corridor, down the south stairs, turned left and headed through the window-lined corridor into the junior high building, which smelled of floorwax, shoepolish, sneakers, lint, and something undefinable, like what was left in the corridor after the living body had gone, permanent, but invisible, like the nonexistent smell of rain coming when skies were clear. Something lasting, what is in that open door? between the eye and the target. Kipling knew—the way explorers know it's Sunday in an alien land.

The kids were all in class so the corridors were empty. I heard a teacher's voice here and there, and getting a sudden whiff of new grass and Missouri earth, flowers budding, in a breeze so soft but fresh it made me dizzy, my heart leaped, I saw that the door was open—the door at the far end of the corridor, and in a soft jewel-like wink, *I was imbued with April.*

Happy, I ducked into the boys' room, went to the far toilet, opened the door, went in, closed it, and knelt by the air vent and lit up *God* that cigarette tasted good! I sat on the floor for a moment, though leaning forward, my elbow on the toilet seat, I inhaled deeply, and exhaled, into the vent. Then I took a puff like my Uncle Fielding, had a conversation with an imaginary audience that was naturally spellbound, and exhaled the plume of smoke into the vent.

The smoke went into the vent like the vent inhaled it, and I had a laughing vision of a wisp of smoke appearing from the chimney at the top of the building.

I had another quick couple of drags, put the butt in the toilet, flushed it down and left, walked down the corridor exhaling hard, and at a blonde-wood door I stopped, and knocked softly. I knew her voice, and when it said come in, I shuddered.

I opened the door and went into the small room, sat at a chair by a desk, and faced her. She sat beside the desk, rather than behind it, and as the desk had been moved sort of to the rear of the small room, it wasn't crowded, and the way it felt was like being with a Sunday school teacher in her work room, although it wasn't like that because it was still school. But it was in school out of school like a relief from it, because I fell in love with the wonderfully pretty woman who was looking at me and smiling. She had the same softness Mother had, and though I knew, and was confused about, what the adults constantly talked about —somebody's age—and how somebody could be older than somebody else but still be young mystified me no end, but I knew she was older than me and younger than Mother, and probably around my sister's age, but I'd never been so close to someone so warm and amused without having been related to them in some way, so my lip-reading teacher was brand new to me so I had a tendency to show off in front of her.

Her eyes were bright, and kind, and smart, too, and her face was open. She had beautiful warm lips, she was like a summer sky, to me, in a soft white blouse with a little blue bow. She had a soft scent which caused my vision to blur a little, and she came through my awe of, and suspense in, her moving life flow like she would cross a field of wildflowers: eyes open and greeny. Me too, I hoped. She had a way of looking at me seriously, though, which I didn't understand, and though she knew I didn't she looked at me that way anyway. As if she was seeing *me*, but that didn't happen often, but when it did I didn't mind. I liked her. I showed her some of my stories. She liked me. She liked my stories, too. She said so.

I put my books on the desk, and without speaking aloud, she moved her welcoming lips silently, saying hello, and I, aloud, responded. Then she asked me how I was, again silently, and I said okay, and then she asked me what I had been doing and I told her, and she responded warmly, and we laughed together, she silently, and when she had paused, and I had gotten ready for what I knew was coming, she silently asked me how about doing the alphabet? I nodded, and she began. A B C D E but then she skipped to fool me and formed the letter P on her lips and smiled, when I laughed at her, saying, aloud,

"P!" and we laughed. She liked music.

So I concentrated on her lips, as she formed M and I said M aloud, and on letters like Y or N or C, she helped by giving them their sequence, like if I couldn't get E she went back to B to C to D, so I could get it, and it was tough, but when I got it she always said, silently:

Good!

and nodded encouragement. Occasionally she talked. And then silently switched to vowels, which were hard, but like playing the extrasensory card games with Mother, I often knew what letter or vowel my lip-reading teacher would form next, and I think she knew I knew, because she got a sharp look in her eyes, and even on her features, as a slight frown, and I knew she knew that I *knew* this wasn't what I should be doing, and I was in my old pattern again, of getting out from what I knew I should be learning, but I—her lips! Her whole self! Tender lips, hard white teeth!

She made a gesture to wait, and sat back and looked at me. I looked back, waiting. Puzzled, but I actually knew, and in me I had a smile ready. So did she, but she also didn't.

She formed, silently: *You*

"You," I said, aloud.

She nodded, *You have*

I—

have

"I can't read you," I said.

She made a gesture with her hand, and briefly shook her head, and silently formed: *You have been—*

"Okay, I see it—I've been—"

Smoking, and she sat back, with a thin smile and angry eyes, as I laughed so spontaneously it startled me, but she shook her head, and a hidden silver angle moved. She pointed to me once, briefly, and said silently, but obviously angry:

You had better watch out!

I nodded, and sat, silently looking at her, as she looked back, eyes flashing.

She was from Cape Girardeau, and had a regular weekly schedule of schools to visit. She lived with her parents, yes she did have a boyfriend, but didn't plan to get married just yet (she wouldn't say any more about it), and as I was curious and jealous she switched the subject and said she wasn't sure if she wanted to go for her Ph.D. or not, and I waited for the knock on the door as she was looking at her watch. She had said some of the things—at first—out loud, but as it went on and the tutorials became more complicated, and I had homework, it was all silent talk on her part, and often I got so involved I answered her likewise silently, and for some reason her eyes got *really* bright, like inside.

I gathered my books up, and stood looking at her warm face, as she smiled, and silently formed her words:

Goodbye, see you next week.

And I left, so dazzled I had to have a quick smoke before I got back to study hall and Mrs. Parham, and reality again, for the few minutes before the study hall bell rang.

You're so lucky, Mother said. This lovely young woman really likes you. She tells me you're doing wonderfully.

"She does?"

"Sure," Mother said, and showed me the note. So there. It was true, for she had written that I was making real progress.

One Fourth of July the Lizard almost blew his thumb off. Lighting two-inchers under tin cans. Which was fun. He arranged a little shelf, or platform, and placed a couple of two-inchers with the fuses tied, under empty Campbell's soup cans. He lit the fuses, and ran back, and in a terrific twin blast we watched the cans take off, and sail end over end up in the air, while the Lizard watched, eyes cobra-sharp, eating the scab from his most recent cut. The day he got hurt he thought the fuse had gone out.

On another Fourth, my Aunty Dot took me to the Fireworks Spectacular at the football stadium at Washington University, and it was a spectacular all right, but not like they planned it, because about five minutes after the show got going (the tame stuff) at the end of "The Star-Spangled Banner," the little shack that held the works at the far end of the field near the goalposts blew up, and it was—incredible. Nobody panicked, everybody clapped and laughed and cheered, nobody was hurt, the racket was terrific, Dorf and me sat there open-mouthed, as the rockets sizzled up in the air, almost cart-wheeled along the whole football field, and red, deep Christmas ornament blue, green, yellow, and silver, blew up before our eyes as tremendous firecrackers sounded all in one long uneven series of explosions, beautiful and wild in outrageous noise and color, while the rockets went crazy, and a few minutes later everybody went home happy.

It was funny, because often the adults enjoyed fireworks like we did, I mean, in the same way, and even before Pearl Harbor, neighbors gave tame but pleasant fireworks displays, and the kids mustn't handle anything *for fear of* aw yeah, and we stood around making faces. It was weird, watching parents lay with miniature sticks of dynamite, faces drawn, and eyes almost glazed, like the Lizard's.

If John Hook had been there he'd have hooked some, sure as sin, which would have guaranteed *our* fun by ourselves on a July tomorrow, because with what he'd hook, and the ones we'd swiped the day before from local stores were bigger and better, it was an exercise in patience to wait until the adults got through with playing, so we could get away into tomorrow, and blast tin cans, go into the tunnel under Taylor Avenue and get half daffy from the echo of cherry bombs. And though it was worth it to wait, it was tough, because we knew what we were going to do—and did do—today, while yesterday we had to wait around and watch the adults have fun, so we could go into action tomorrow.

When I woke on summer mornings, and today had become tomorrow, and I raised the blind and looked out my window and saw the cistern standing before the crabapple tree beyond, my mind went into a swoop at what I could do, and as the sunlight twinkled off the treetops, and down through the leaves onto the grass and flowers in the Pickles' next door lot, I knew I'd play some Indian ball, or go swimming at the pool with Danny Hoffman, or go for a long hike, write a story about home and maybe draw a little, because the sight of that pure midwestern sky drew me outward into what a great day it was for a ballgame, and I lay in bed in suspense, and in bewildered awe at how yesterday's present had become tomorrow's today, during the night, which I knew would continue, which is how I learned to trust the future, in a thrill that made me dizzy —no, *dizzier.*

My Uncle Fielding (Fee), was the president of a company that made gummed and ungummed gift stickers, stamps, and seals. He and his wife, my Aunt Emily, and their daughter, my cousin Carol, lived in Peoria, where he worked and she (Aunt Emily) taught grammar school.

We got a lot of free Christmas stickers every year.

Uncle Fee, Aunt Em, and Cousin Carol visited us at least twice a year, and at least once a year they came with the newest collection of slides taken on their most recent vacation in Mexico.

Uncle Fee, to whom Mouse spoke much as to myself, I mean, he said Hiya Feelin', which greeting included most everything, and as they were brothers who had grown up together, Uncle Fee knew what Uncle Mouse meant. But Mouse's brothers and sisters called him Es—short for Essex —and in fact except for the kids in the neighborhood and the people in my house, nobody called Mouse Mouse: five feet three, thin, too thin, perhaps, and he had his father's head, the family eyes and lips, and he had the mustache that was popular then, a small chunk of hair below the nose. After the First War, when my father was in Poland working with homeless orphans for the Red Cross, he had a mustache like that too (I saw the photographs), so the real reason Hitler had the same kind was because it was still popular.

But Fee was the most dapper of my uncles, and it probably was because he had more money, although he didn't behave in any pre-ten-tious way: he dressed, walked, sat, stood, and looked and did everything but talk like an executive, and in the way he saw me and we'd played tiddlywinks when I was little, and he enjoyed, it seemed, beating me, I felt he was an executive in the way he could spot me, bingo! with his dark and quiet eyes, I never felt he looked down on me, and in fact I never felt that about any of my aunts and uncles except Aunt Emily, but then she was a teacher. Anyway I liked Uncle Fielding because I was his namesake, and he talked the same way to everybody. I think that too was a characteristic of my aunts and uncles, except Aunt Emily, but then she taught Spanish, and I heard she was pretty strict. I also heard she was dedicated.

So in spite of how I generally saw everything and everyone through my fog, Uncle Fielding and Aunt Em were two adults who stood straight up and straight ahead in my head, and in my memory.

(Not like Uncle Brent, who was not my uncle, and whose middle name should have been Sideways, as he came up the sidewalk and everyone sighed as his tired figure came up the steps onto the porch and joined my mother and my aunts there, for a glass of iced tea, and some idle conversation. Uncle Brent fascinated me, he was the world to me, the daily double, the odds in the 6th, in his tired, slow vanishing sideways style, and thinness, like really old politicians, because when he saw me he smiled his yesteryear racetrack smile, and said huskily, Hiya Seabiscuit!)

(I saw him in the crowd, with a woman in a yellow dress, and himself in a seersucker summer suit, and straw hat down over his eyes, cigarette tilting up as he laughed, and his eyes narrowed to her)

A dear man? A past rascal, they said. I came into the living room.

Uncle Fee said, Here he is.

We shook hands, and he looked at me, as I stood before him in my short pants and shirt, and he said,

Well, you look pretty good. Better than what I've been hearing, anyway (as my face clouded), he laughed and his rimless glasses twinkled. I'm only kidding, he said. Don't be so serious.

He was thin, but for some reason looked plump. He was the kind of man who could (and did) wear vests and look great. He had a warm, very pleasant face, a brief hairline mustache, and as his hair was thinning, he looked, every inch of him, like a happy banker.

He didn't talk much, he left that to Aunt Emily, and when asked, he sounded syllables like Mouse, he knew what brevity was, and in fact too much talk by too many people (one too many would do it if one other person was talking), irritated him, and it somehow always seemed because he was impatient. Like Mouse, and maybe all my uncles, he didn't like long explanations, and when he got either angry or impatient or both, a certain hard-edged Missouri twang came out of his throat, and people sort of jumped, and after everybody had done what he wanted, very little, he sat there in quiet control, because he was, like all my uncles, shy, and self-effacing, and literally (almost) wouldn't hurt a fly.

Anyway, I liked him, and sat so I could watch him and if possible be near him, as he sipped coffee, and smoked. He was handsome, and had the family head, but his face seemed round to me, and as he sat there, in himself, and quiet and listening, he seemed to be amused by it all, and that wasn't true, because he listened with a good deal of care, and often interjected idle comments, as became the President of the Company.

But the way he smoked!

He held the cigarette between and near the tips of his index and middle finger, and placing it carefully between his lips, the palm of his hand facing his throat, he inhaled so effortlessly it seemed he wasn't, and after he lowered his hand as he listened or talked as Emily came into the living room and sat down and got into the conversation and even if he was speaking, however briefly, no smoke came out, and as his hands were crossed on his knee (which was crossed over his leg), the room went into the state of refraction, and I sat transfixed. No smoke came out! *I've got to learn that,* I thought, and watched him the way Lizard watched the fuses of two-inchers and the way Aunty Dot made her gruesome special diet suppers of boiled bananas, or the way she listened to Bob Hope on the radio, and my sister Ca and me listened too: the comic man said, to Frances Langford,

Put your hand in my pocket

But Bob, I feel so silly!

Go in a little deeper, he said, and you'll feel nuts, and fifty million Americans laughed with Dorf, who said Isn't he *awful?*

And when Uncle Fee lit up I went into a sort of cosmic suspense, and sat, hands gripping my kneecaps, and probably with my mouth open, but my eyes were absolutely FIXED on his lips as he inhaled—in his inhalation I was nearly drawn off the chair, I often coughed, I didn't smoke like that and his dry run made me choke, and once, unable to control myself, I asked him how he did it.

"WHAT!?" coughed smoke. I must have got him at the wrong point, and after he wiped his eyes he asked me what in hell I was talking about, and not to do that while he was smoking.

I apologized, and didn't do it again, but I watched and in the basement and in the garage practiced until I could do it, and though it took concentration, I did. I said, to my pals,

Okay this is how my Uncle Fee smokes.

I crossed my legs, I had their attention, and I sat back against the tree, held the Chesterfield between my two fingers, and raising it to my lips, took (to them) an almost secret puff, and after I inhaled, I looked at them calmly, and said something or other about someone or other, discussed the latest baseball averages of my favorite players until they were getting interested, and as they began to lean toward me, eyes wide, I blew a long, thin plume of smoke in their faces.

I could imitate Mouse, too. It was me who got everybody saying "bunk."

I could in fact do anything I put my mind to except homework which I did not put my mind to, which is why I flunked, and which was not funny, which is why Mouse told me to do it, Goddammit just do it and get it over with, you're makin' your mother miserable.

I sat in back of the projector, and watched the slides Aunt Emily had recently taken in Mexico. I watched my Uncle Fee blow plumes of smoke, as Uncle Mouse puffed Wings cigarettes (with an airplane card on every pack: small, blue silver skyline wings: a GEE BEE on the runway!), and as Mouse flicked an occasional ash off his knee, tilted his head and looked at the slides saying nothing, me and Ca knew he was a really good photographer, and was being patient with Aunt Emily while she lectured us. Her pictures, with a slide here and there of Uncle Fee standing in the plaza in front of a church, were good, too, some were terrific, she knew what she was talking about, pronounced those names with the q's and x's like it surely was, and as she talked and we looked and listened, Carol slept upstairs on Aunt Dorf's bed, as Aunty Mary fiddled with her hearing aid as Emily pointed out tombs, monuments, churches, mountains, glyphs, and natives in their native dress, and discussed their customs and language, and her voice went in and got stuck in my head not to be forgotten, because she enjoyed what she was talking about because she knew it, and though she regarded me as someone who stood a pretty good chance of getting in her way (I stayed out of her way), she went right on, Damn, as Aunty Mary would say, the torpedoes, a warm, full-bodied, sharp, smart, sensible, businesslike breezy bossy professional woman —telling us where they went and what they did, in Mexico, under *those* blue skies. Full speed ahead.

So, after they left, and drove back to Peoria, they were a topic of discussion, when I wasn't around, or wasn't supposed to be around, to hear, but did anyway.

All that makeup!

And how she picks on Fielding! It isn't fair!

Well, they love each other, Mother said, poising a big fat question mark in my head, as my sister Ca said to everybody, about Aunt Emily,

"You're just jealous of her"—in a sudden storm of protest why we *love* Emily! How can you—even—

"Old Meh-hee-co," Mouse smiled: and Emily. Boy oh boy.

Mrs. Gamble lived across the street, and she was Mary Morris's mother. I was in love with Mary Morris because she looked so royal the way she walked and talked. The Gambles were from the South, and were related to President Tyler I think, and on Sunday evenings Mrs. Gamble invited the kids to come over and listen to *The Hound of the Baskervilles* which we did, and boy, I mean it scared the daylights outa us, I R A N across the street home: poor Lizard, Wimp, Cissie, Steve, Hobey, and Jan, who had to walk home the long way and under all those trees, too. *Hearing the hound bay.*

But to wait a whole week to listen again was unbearable.

Anyway, one afternoon I was walking down the middle of Taylor Avenue singing my usual, "The Battle Hymn of the Republic," and Mrs. Gamble appeared on her front porch and called a rather soft arc to me, to come to her, and as I approached she asked if I wanted to come in and have a sandwich, so I said sure (suspecting something), and we went in. She led me back to the kitchen with her hand on my shoulder, she more sailed than walked, and as she began to prepare the sandwich, she said she was going to make me a peanut butter sandwich like they have down south, with mayonnaise, had I ever had that? No, I said, respectfully, and she put it together, cut it in half, put it on a plate, folded a paper napkin beside it, poured a glass of cold milk, and we sat at the kitchen table, and she said, in her soft, aristocratic way that meant that portrait of President Tyler over the fireplace wasn't a joke,

Fieldin' darlin', couldn't you sing "Dixie," instead of that *otha* song?

I laughed, thinking I'd tell Mother that and said sure, biting into the sandwich, which had a pretty weird taste, and I wasn't sure if I liked it, but I drank some milk and took another bite. She watched me, thinking of her song, I thought.

"Don't you like it?" she asked.

I blinked. "Which?"

She put her hand to the pearls at her throat, tilted her head back and laughed. Ah ah, she said. That's good. The *sandwich*, dear boy!

Chewing, I looked out the window onto Orrick Lane, and sighed, "Yes, it's good," I said. What a liar.

Mother was amused. You didn't have to lie, she said. Mary Lyon's a wonderful and honest woman.

We were at supper. I looked at Mouse, who didn't say anything, some pal, and Aunty Mary asked for the peas mmp, as Aunty Katie and Aunty Mil were having a tug of war for the margarine I'd mixed.

Mouse laughed, and said, You think he's gonna tell Mary Lyon it was no good? She knows the songs she likes to hear.

Aunty Dot yelled: WHAT?

It was different, I said.

My sister slowly winked one eye and looked up at the ceiling.

What was different? Mother asked.

The sandwich. That's what I should have said. It was different.

Did you like it? Mouse asked.

No, I laughed.

Mother looked perplexed, amused, and a little irritated, and my sister said what was really different was this war, not that one, and in all the shouting and eating it took us a while to figure out she meant the Second one, not Mary Lyon's.

As I went in the front door of the house I faced the stairs to the second floor. To the right was the living room, and beyond it the library. To the left the dining room and beyond it the kitchen.

Mother's room was above the dining room. Dorf's room was above the living room. Mary's room was above the library and Mil's room was above the kitchen, with a back stairs down which the weekly laundry was thrown.

The room Mouse and I shared was in back, reached by a small hallway, that led to or from the kitchen or library. At the other end of the hall was our small bathroom.

So, when Aunty Katie broke her hip she moved out of Aunty Mil's room, which they'd shared, and into the dining room, which meant the dining room and the library changed places. That meant that Aunty Katie would (and did) use the same bathroom that me and Mouse did. It also meant that I had to be careful when I snuck into the kitchen for a late-night snack, so as not to wake her, as she had to get up and go to work, broken hip or no, and it—whatever noise I made—didn't make her cranky, it made her ANGRY GO: to BED Fee, in a growl that spun into a wailcry: IT'S TOO LATE!

(Sunday afternoon)

Essex, you *must* tell him—

Yeah, okay.

Feeee! Dorf cried (from upstairs). Where's Fee? KAY! is FEE down there?

Mouse and Katie looked at each other.

NO DOROTHY, shouted Katie. He's UP ON MATTHEWS' FIELD!

Where? WHAT? yelled Aunty Dot, moving around to the top of the stairs.

Mouse pointed north, and said, angrily and a little disgustedly, He's up on Matthews' Field. HE'S UP ON MATTHEWS'—Aunty Katie yelled. Oh well, I *heard* you, you don't have to yell, Dorf said, as I came into view from the living room—Oh there he is, cried Dorf, and she laughed as Katie furiously looked at me mumbling *Dorothy* with a couple of repeats as Mouse laughed angrily and shook his head, saying to me as he went into the living room, What in hell are you doin' here.

Aunty Dot disappeared into her room and I heard her say come *on,* so I went up the steps as Katie hobbled back into her room. Through the fog blowing over my essential common sense, I sensed a warm silliness. I reached the top step, turned right, and as I faced the doorway to Aunty Mary's room, I was facing north, so turning right and going up a couple of more steps, I faced east and walked down the small hall to Dorf's room on the left, across the hall from Mother's and Ca's room. I passed the bathroom as I went, where I often spied on my sister through the keyhole, as she dried herself after baths. I turned left into my Aunt Dorothy's room.

She had the closet door open, and stood, pencil in hand, waiting for me. I took off my shoes, and in stocking feet stood against the doorjamb. She pushed my shoulders back and chest in, and made sure my head was against the wood.

She made the mark, wrote the date, and stepped back, saying well, not much.

Maybe a quarter of an inch. Let's measure it!

She quickly crossed her room, opened a drawer, fumbled around and pulled out a cloth tape, returned to me, and after a few seconds of calculation, asked that I stand up straight again, she pushing me around a little, but after she got me all fixed, as I looked out the window and sighed, watching the sun hit the trees in the color contrast with black asphalt along that part of the Gambles' lawn to the distant white façade of the Brauns' house through the trees, Dorf said okay, good, and fixing her bifocals as she slightly bent, murmured a little over one-eighth exactly, she stepped back, looked at me, and grinned.

Well, she sang, with her high-pitched gaiety: You're still GROWWWWWIIINNNG!

I sat on the floor and put my shoes on.

She closed the door to her room, sat at her desk, and after putting the pencil and tape on top, rummaged around and took a thick book in her hands, as I said, Aw come on, Dorf. Please.

Listen, she said, opening *Gray's Anatomy*, as long as nobody else is telling you, I will. You've got to know—you probably already do, but I'M GOING TO TELL YOU ANYWAY!!!

She pointed to a precise medical drawing in different colors of an erect penis, and as I was saying Aw gee whiz, etc., she said you know what that is and I said yeah.

She turned a few pages, and showed me a multicolored precision drawing of a vagina, and I nodded, embarrassed, beginning to think maybe I should turn away.

This—LOOK at it, she said. This is the clitoris and this—

If left, hearing her laugh, a little guiltily, saying well this is being *mod*-ern, and I want to *help*, and if Essex won't, somebody should.

Mother, always, was angry, by having realized where I was in the geography of the house, and lip-reading the look on my face, like a common-sense Mother-intuition: *Dorf?* I nodded. *Again?* I nodded, and she laughed angrily. Footsteps.

DOROTHY, *leave* him *alone!*

He's *got* to know, she said, stoutly.

But *you* don't have to teach him!

*Some*body should!

Can't you see how it embarrasses him?

Oh fiddlesticks.

If he wants to know, Mother shouted: HE'LL ASK ESSEX!

He won't! HE KNOWS HOW SHY ESSEX IS!

Well, don't *you* tell him.

Fumes and turmoil. Footsteps receding, offstage. Other steps.

Essex, you've got to explain things to Fee. Dorothy's been at it again.

Yeah, I know. And maybe he does too.

Those things, yes, but not other things, she said. *Why* does she *persist?*

He chuckled and said something I didn't hear. Mother said, Well that may be, but he's going to think of sex as dirty, and she's not helping any.

That's true, Mouse admitted. Okay, I'll talk with him.

That night after supper while I was listening to the radio, Mouse cleared his throat. He was working on his stamp collection, and he said something about my father not being here anymore, and my mother having it tough being alone these days, and if there were things I wanted to know I could ask him.

Okay, I said. I will, wings fluttering. It's just that when Dorf—

Yeah, he nodded, missing my vindication: it's embarrassing.

So later that night, like most every night, when he and Frances (his sweetheart), were out together, I lay in bed and looked out the open window at the cistern, the crab apple tree, and the trees and bushes alongside Pickles' back lot and alone in a way I liked, quickly jacked off, and a while later, again—days I missed, I caught up with the next day— thinking of a girl who lived in a white house down the street, and of the real vagina in that medical drawing on my mind.

When we came to Kirkwood, Mother had to get a job, so she got the job as secretary to the minister of the Episcopal church. The parish house, where she worked, was a block away, on the corner of Washington and Taylor, so while Daddy had been in New York she was working for the church, and after he died, she stayed on. I didn't mind. Something new! and I learned a lot. I liked having her near, although passing the parish house coming and going to and from Pitman occasionally made me self-conscious, and embarrassed, for some reason, which irritated me, and ashamed, I went home the other way—down Kirkwood Road to Bodley, right on Bodley and then right on Taylor across from Matthews' Field and in front of Matthews' big house, and came home down Taylor.

That was the way, and my favorite way, I went when I sang "The Battle Hymn of the Republic"—walking down the middle of the street.

When I did pass the parish house, though, without fail I'd call up to her, that's where her office was, and the second floor window opened and her gorgeous face appeared, and my heart almost burst as we called and waved hello and exchanged the news, before I waved so long and turned left for home.

"Fee, where were you today? I missed you!"

That's when I had gone the other way.

The door opened. Footsteps.

Just getting the worst, murmured Aunty Mil, coming into the room.

Saturday morning. Viola was off. Mouse up, and into the country with Frances. 8:30 a.m.

Aw, Aunty Mil, why so *early,* I said, furiously, waking myself up, digging back in under the covers, and turning my deaf (right) ear to the world, not so quickly, however, as to miss hearing her say, as she always did, in a happy chuckle,

It won't take but a minute, and then you can go back to sleep. Dust mop.

Click and whsh.

The door to the cellar was in my room, and every day Aunty Mary came down the hall from the kitchen, down the one step into our room (Mouse was away at work so it was me alone, and as Mother came in to say hi, after work, every day, the foggy hour and a half I had to myself after school was interrupted by Aunty Mary), and crossing the room she went into the cellar for potatoes, onions, etc., for supper. She turned her hearing aid off so she couldn't hear me when I yelled at her, in my continuing fight for privacy. The door to the room didn't have a lock, and even if it had, the house had settled in such a way the door couldn't close, and in the smoke of my fury I never had the clear thought to take it off its hinges and plane it down to make it crooked so it would fit the crooked jamb. Then put a lock on it. She would have been *forced* to knock, which would have infuriated her as, she often said, as mulish as me, more mulish in fact, it was her kitchen and she needed things to make supper in her kitchen, therefore access to the cellar was her right no matter how unfair I thought it was.

I was often so angry I couldn't think, and wanted to hit her as much to clear my head as to hurt her, but I couldn't do that, so I fumed and screamed—

YOU NEVER *ASK!* I shouted, feeling a rising rage, hands shaking.

"I have to get supper," she clipped, and brushed by me, opening the cellar door and disappearing down the old wooden steps, and I heard her rooting around.

I went around in circles unable to breathe right, deeply sighing with my hands in fists, to *kill,* one *hit* to kill and when she came up, I yelled, near tears, splitting:

HITLER! YOU'RE A LITTLE HITLER! The hit in Hitler. I liked: liked it, loved it, jacked off in it, the hit. Her. Hitter.

"Say what you please," she said, smugly quoting the 19th century, "I have to make supper," and she briskly left the room, the goods in her arms.

It brought me near blackout. My heart beat my temples rang and my head crashed between tears and murder with no place to go. I threw myself on the bed and kicked my legs, beat the pillows with my fists and screamed into the blankets.

But then, in the nonviolent Episcopal Sunday afternoon character of home, feelings were moods that changed, and it was a surprise to us all when my, or my sister's, rage appeared, and revenge hit home, my guilt equalled Aunty Mary's hurt, as out of control, fury unleashed and my eyes blazed as I cursed her *Nazi, Fascist, Hitler*—a WOMAN HITLER, she wept, frightened, saying she was a pacifist, and violence was wrong, I shouldn't say things like that, and while I suffered reprimands from Aunty Katie, or whoever caught me when I was enraged with Aunty Mary, inside myself I turned inside out, and my blood ran white in shame, and trapped frustration, as a pulpy gorge rose in my throat if I could have I would have *vomited* semen.

All I had was words, and I didn't know the right ones which were the forbidden ones, and when I did I was too angry to say them. At supper, other fighting broke out, as Aunty Katie, who was forking chunks of overcooked fish into her mouth, spoke, with mouth full MARY

MARY DON'T EAT SO FAST! WATCH OUT FOR THE BONES!

What? asked Aunty Mary, fiddling with her hearing aid, having forgotten to turn it up.

WATCH OUT FOR THE BONES! yelled Aunty Dot.

Dorothy, Mother said.

WELL, Aunty Dot shrieked at Mother, DO YOU WANT HER TO CHOKE?

Aunty Katie nodded, and Mother said, diplomatically, but getting really angry, Of course not. Why do you always have to YELL?

Because she's deaf, said Aunty Mil, and Mouse said because she's deaf: BECAUSE SHE'S DEAF, Dorf shouted.

So are you, I said, and my sister and I laughed, and Dorothy, getting red, having heard that, and her sense of humor cutting in on her anger, looked like she was going to call the fire department, and not on the telephone, said, in her hurt, which shamed me: Yes, and then leveled out in anger again, But *not like MARY!*

Nobody's deaf like Mary, Aunty Mil chirped a grin, and everybody laughed, including Mary, only the variations were different, Pass the spinach, said Aunty Katie, and Dorothy passed it to her as I squeezed more lemon on my fish, and Dorf reached across in front of my sister and took a lemon slice.

DOROTHY! (all) Shocked.

Oh who cares, Dorf snapped, and I ate my supper as

they quarreled and quibbled, and passed food back and forth to each other, often almost slinging it. I mashed up the lumpy potatoes that were lumpy because I hadn't beat 'em up right, and I put on a big scoop of the oleo I had mixed right, a lot of salt and more pepper, and mixed in some fish chips and some of the overcooked spinach, and washed it all down with milk, and after I took care of the tapioca with a nibble or two, I was finished. Everybody angrily helped clean up, almost dropping, or tossing, the dishes into the sink, and walking out to have coffee on the front porch to forget what just happened, leaving whoever it was in the rotation to do the dishes, which person, in a near homicidal rage, nearly weeping, but did do them, which is why the plates, glasses, and silverware always had a kind of greasy speckled look, and when it came my turn, the easiest way out was break all the plates and glasses, and along with the silverware, throw it all in the garbage. Well. Okay. The task that was ours to do—my sister and I—was to wipe off, gather, and put away the placemats, wipe off the table and straighten out the chairs, and because supper was eaten in its normal fury (some meals were quiet), the floor was invariably a mess, and had to be swept, so instead of wiping the table and then cleaning the floor, we wiped crumbs and the different sized bits of food onto the floor, and then swept the floor. I wasn't amused. All told, when the whole mess was cleaned up, it was disgusting. Ca and I agreed: These women pigs.

I was clipping grass along the edges of the front walk, when I saw Gus coming up the sidewalk. Tired, stoop-shouldered, and heading home.

"Gus!" I called, to his shaggy, bent figure. His old eyes peered at me from under the brim of his floppy hat. A large old animal.

"How can you tell if it's gonna rain?"

"If the clouds are low, and you can smell the damp in the air. No dew on the grass the night before," he said, patiently. "That's when there's clouds. But if it's a clear night the moon'll have a ring around it."

I blinked, and looked at him amazed. He smiled, in the way a *bison* smiles, and I thanked him as he slowly went his way.

Bob Howell's father's hardware store was on the west side of Kirkwood Road, across, and on the south side of the Missouri-Pacific Railroad tracks, almost opposite the railroad station and therefore in the heart of town.

Railway sidings swept along the tracks for a few miles east and west, so walking to and from junior high school, I'd often pass rows of parked boxcars, engines, tenders, and cabooses.

Kirkwood had originated because it was the first railway stop west of St. Louis, and for many years was, after stops had been designated between Kirkwood and St. Louis, an end of the line for commuters, so there was a roundhouse. It was huge, dark, and blazed the sight and sound of sparkblast in a screech of steel, as the engines turned around, which was especially thrilling at night. After westward expansion began taking place, and Kirkwood lost its original value to the railroad, the roundhouse was torn down and a small park was made, a town flagpole was raised, and the view was very pleasant and irrelevant. But the sidings remained, and an air of old railroad days clung to the area, and made it hard for anybody to forget, although the next generation wouldn't know the dif.

I had loved watching the engines in slow spin. The roundhouse was a massive, dark, awkward, filthy menace of a structure with a great, deep-girdered, flattop iron turntable with glistening silver rails on which the engine rested, like a mechanical cow turning round under the glare of hundreds of naked white bulbs, and the steady sound, deeper, more contained than an earthquake, blended with the screams of thousands of small, mechanical insects, blue smoke, stink of grease, coal-fire and electricity in an occasional whiff of the hills and woods nearby.

When Mother or Mouse or Aunty Katie needed something to fix something, I was often asked to run down to Kirkwood for it. Or, on the way home from school, Fee, pick up six screws *just like this:* and she'd place a small brass screw in my hand.

We also used Rott Hardware, which was closer, but Bob Howell's dad had a better selection and, as I always thought, better stock.

The old roundhouse had been diagonally across the tracks from the hardware store, and facing south on this side of the tracks and to the left of the train station. The new park was parallel with Argonne Drive as well as the tracks. Argonne Drive went east and west, and was divided in the center by a two-hundred-yard-long grassy island, and there were some tombstones and a monument to the men who had fallen in the First World War, and it was on that island that the American Legion Carnival was held every summer, so when the roundhouse was torn down it made more room for the American Legion Carnival idea.

In those summer carnival months I went into my haze —a special one that kept me betwixt and between, and I drifted and dreamed in a semi-articulate state and was hardly aware of anything and I could walk along and be alone in fields or alongside highways without a care in the world.

Lighthearted.

And carefree in my little dizziness on the warm skyblue 1944 June afternoon I walked out of Howell's hardware store, went down the steps, jaywalked east across Kirkwood Road, and headed north across the tracks, and as I did so I saw a man up ahead, standing beside a flatcar stacked with watermelons. He was slender and pale, in dark raggedy clothes, and as his eyes fell on me I cringed under his haunted and unhappy gaze. Almost before our eyes had met, I felt him struggling within, I kept walking, almost stumbling, eyes lowered, to go by him. But he was an invisible wall of force, and he took a step to intercept me as I walked faster ducking out of his way, I saw his pale hand reach, in tattered white cuff, as he said,

"Son—could, would you do me a favor?"

Then I looked at him, his lean frame and pale unshaven face—and his eyes! as if bled into me, his eyes were as clear as what he wanted, which caught my breath in terror as I felt myself leap from my skin and flee across the tracks, as his husky voice pleaded, and both his hands gestured—

Make a sign for me, son: *"Watermelons For Sale."*

I—I—and he stopped, lowered his eyes, and bit his lip.

I can't write. Make a sign for me son, please.

I stood before him paralyzed as he held out a piece of battered cardboard and a chewed pencilstub, his voice was —horrible, and yet he seemed to know me clear through, and could within me touch me almost as no other could. My heart stopped and I shrank back, as he softly pleaded,

You can do it. You know how. I can see you know how!

He smiled, and his eyes twinkled in some cosmic wisdom and I almost screamed. I looked at him wild-eyed, as his wise and kind eyes gazed in mine

DO IT! a voice yelled.

Please, son.

No! I choked, shaking my head, feeling him struggle, and I—I *ran.* Across the tracks where I turned right on Argonne, and ran east, pausing for a moment and sending a furtive glance over my shoulder. My eyes met his long clear gaze, following me, as he stood by the tracks back there by the flatcar, in dejection, with the cardboard and shattered pencil in his hands, staring at me, figure hollow in rejection.

I got home breathless, anxious, frightened, and guilty, and in a desperate need toward a larger force I had to tell somebody so I searched for and found my sister, and I told her I told her I did something wrong but I couldn't help it and she looked at me.

So I told her, my eyes avoiding hers.

In that way she had of anger combined with grief, she whispered *You.*

You, she continued, *you* above ALL PEOPLE would, and she said it as from the dungeons of us: would *deny a poor man*. You, she pointed (at me),

Go back and *make that SIGN!*

I well I ran up Taylor to Argonne, went right along it and turned left on Kirkwood Road, ran across the tracks and the watermelon man was gone. Tacked onto the flatcar was a sign on white cardboard, with bold lettering: Watermelons For Sale,

I told her, hanging my head, and she said that poor guy, and my throat tightened.

Why couldn't you? she asked

I—I don't know, I stammered, I *couldn't,* I laughed, NO! I cried, remembering him, and his pleading warm eyes, they almost *burned* me. BURNED ME I can see you—*I see you know how.* He had—seen, me. Known! How had he seen?

I said, desperately, He said he knew I could write.

You knew he knew! she cried, look at you! Couldn't you have done it for *him?*

It, it wasn't that it was for him, I blurted. I don't know, and I hung my head, and then I laughed hysterically—*I couldn't,* he was—

She nodded, then, and I knew what she meant. Florida, Pittsburgh, and all the very very poor along the way... My body rocked in conflict, as I stared at the floor, not daring to meet her eyes.

On Halloween Mother said, Let's play a joke on Mouse, and when she told me, I was enthusiastic, so we dressed me up as a girl, and briefed everybody but Mouse, so at supper, there I was with everybody else at the table, in my bandanna, calico dress, lipstick, and rouge, sitting next to Mouse as Mother explained I was an orphan girl who had come by the parish house in desperation and Mother had invited her to supper, isn't she pretty? My aunts and me kept our heads down to keep from laughing, I could hardly control myself it was so funny, and Mouse sat there eating his supper, embarrassed, thinking everybody was weeping, and as the meal went on the impact changed—I couldn't say anything because he'd know my voice—and within myself I began to wonder what was going on. I didn't want to hurt him, and I felt an odd panic, *It's a joke, Mouse, we don't mean to*— and yet in the wild fun I laughed so much tears were in my eyes, and my throat hurt as I looked at Mother, and she caught an inner imploring gaze in the center of the amusement and hysteria, and then unable to carry it on everybody laughed and the girl was unveiled as Fee.

Unh huh, he said softly, ya didn't fool me. But she had fooled him.

I laughed, glad, but I was confused—and angry—and I said, blurted out—

I didn't?

You think I don't know ya?

And as I laughed in relief, I was angry—he wouldn't admit he was fooled, and though I loved him for it, there was something I couldn't figure out, and in a way I had been fooled by him, and he had fooled me.

Not at first, though. Yet somebody had fooled me.

Then we had dessert. Tapioca. I could hardly get it down, yet I was delighted by the mystery. And the joke at first.

I went upstairs to ask Mother for some money for the movies, and she was sitting at her dresser before her mirror, combing her long white hair. I stood behind her, looking into the mirror. It was like a game, and something we did often, which warmed my heart and me from top to bottom, also made me a wee bit tipsy, she was so beautiful.

As I parted my lips to speak, she sang the lyric with a gleam in her eye,

> Rapunzel, Rapunzel
> Let down your golden hair

Her own long and silver hair that reached her waist, as she raised her arms, and combed, and combed, as I watched, enthralled.

The fog comes in
On big soft feet.
It smells of tin
And looks down the street.

John South and I skipped school and hitchhiked out to the Meramec River. May, 1945.

It was fun, daring to skip, and then see the river. Take off after lunch. We didn't skip often, all told about three or four afternoons. Always in a heightened sense of adventure into space—along Kirkwood Road to Highway 66, and then down to Valley Park, and from there we walked to the river.

Valley Park was a mill town, and the one large mill supported about fifteen hundred families. John and I walked along the hot, dry, bleak sidewalks looking in dusty windows at dusty merchandise and cheap secondhand clothes, and at men on the streets who looked like ghosts in the sunshine.

There wasn't even a movie house.

We passed a couple of gas stations, with their piles of useless tires, junk, and parked banged-up cars, as farmers and poor people stood around the Coke machine, defeated and almost transparent, rolling cigarettes and listening to the gas station radio.

We walked up a dirt road, over a small shady hillock and down to the level, dried, mud-covered riverside: splintered twigs, sticks, logs, smashed bushes and grass, scattered broken beer and soda bottles, in the feel of a mud-coated once-great waterworld drained, leaving its open floor to the sun. Tree trunks crusted twenty feet up, an occasional abandoned summer cottage, silent and without echo or sound, save the soft whisper of the low Meramec beyond, and we walked along that shore, skipping stones, sending sticks cartwheeling into water—near the wharf I found a tortoise shell picked clean, which I rubbed off, to gaze at its hidden glossy design, as in a thrum from the bottom of a different river—with a snarl John snatched it away, threw it into the river, a bad throw, it fell short, not far from our feet, and before I knew it he, then we, were on top of the wharf, shirts off, side by side on our stomachs smoking cigarettes, watching poor kids across the river, at the foot of their shabby, broken wooden houses on stilts because of heavy flood waters, listening to their outcries, screams and whoops, as they paddled and swam in muddy water.

John was taller, had red hair, a pink rather cruel face, freckles, rotten teeth, and a continuous infectious nasty laugh in his throat, he ate Ex-lax like candy.

His chest was hollow-ribbed, skin as white as clabber, hairless armpits lined with dirt, the nape of his scrawny neck grimy into his hair. His shoulders sloped into blue-veined arms and wrists, large freckled hands and blunt fingers like mitts, dirty nails cracked. His mouth was a liquid blur, his nose a smudge. His heavy-lidded, unnerving blue eyes prone to sidelong glances—not at me—right through me. Who was I? He didn't care. I liked that. I liked him. One day I sucked his dick.

We walked along the riverbank, he seemed moody, seizing stones I wanted to skip and he did not at all, for he threw them down, hard, into the shallows to make a splash . . . over a hill, under trees . . . we stopped at a gas station and had Cokes.

As we hitchhiked home, John opened another box of Ex-lax, and ate the whole thing as I stood on the edge of Highway 66 grinning at him, John! you're gonna shit in your pants!

His eyes twinkled and he grinned, and bared his rotten teeth—Think so? he laughed nastily, he was from the South, and it went kind of like this: oh ah jest *loves* that!

And we were giddy, he was so crazy, as I drew looks from other boys when I kept in John's company, and they made hints to me, so when John quit school the next year and moved away I was glad, yet I missed him.

They asked me what John and I did together when we skipped, and I lied in a way that made them laugh, because they were liars too, and it was funny all around, in a hard laugh, just this side of a sneer, but too close to almost going out of control, I *had* to guard my secret and I worried about those boys who approached me as I put my books in my locker, or mid-stride along the jammed corridors I got to know their secret looks, anyway, I lived in a fear, and once in a while they chased me as I chased them and they chased themselves and everybody chased everybody and tripped me like they tripped each other, but as my legs were still weak from the accident, I couldn't run, and when, worst of all, the biggest bullies on the football team corked my arm and grinned hello, I cringed and cowered before them, hating the sight of them with a hatred that struck green-gold sparks from a loathing that left me weak, vulnerable, and half crazy from fantasies of revenge, which in one mad morning I actuated. I put thumbtacks, points out, through a patch of adhesive tape, plastering it to my arm, which worked, and though in my cowardice I was humiliated, and though my arm got bruised, it was a thrill to see the bullies cry out in pain and suck their knuckles, as I vanished into the throng in the corridor, running away. I always ran away. Almost always.

I ran from every fight, and those I was in I lost, and that isn't true, but I clowned and laughed and stammered and flunked in fear, wishing I could turn into a killer of bullies, those bullies that picked on everybody smaller than they, and never, ever, on anyone their size, and yet as I ran from them I could only run to a point which demanded I turn and chase, but that point was so far away, and it was as if I had to run through so much fog and confusion to enter the strength where I could challenge, I was exhausted before

I fled. I wasn't a selected victim, because bullies picked on anybody smaller who happened to be in their vicinity, and what was really crazy was, the more I avoided 'em the more bully-ish they got and it was like at church, they wanted their victims to understand them, which I could do and was the reason I was a favorite among the bullies, depending on their mood, because while they pestered me they knew I understood, and,—it was so confusing! because, and I wasn't alone, no, never, there were lots like me and it was as if we lived in a perpetual victimized understanding of all the bullies in school, and at the big football games, particularly the Turkeyday game, there we were, out there cheering for those bullies! H'ray!

Thinking of phrases of praise, in the (certain) event of future encounters with them.

The girls knew, too, the ones that mattered, anyway, and you bet your bottom dollar—they sure were glad they weren't boys!

My daydreams of murder. If I was Superman, if *I* was Captain Nemo, *that* football player would be stretched and strung out in bloody pieces by my own happy hand from Kirkwood to Kansas City.

Daydreams and nightdreams of being pursued, and those awful eyes burning out at me, and the air seemed damp and inwardly twisted, as a gasping torque out of the center of which shone one deadly eye. All dream, hallucination, day or night, All non-substance in the Substance, and I felt strong bonds to the night in the day and to the bright fact of brilliant night, and the felt or sensed reversal in my mind, which I wondered if I was losing, so afraid to see the world, yet so unafraid, to see the world I loved I made a world I loved, and I began to shift to feeling through a fog, a daze, so I wouldn't have to respond to it direct. If I could feel without responding, wasn't that vague? and I wanted that certification of vagueness, because it seemed that a haze or a fog or vagueness was as clear as day or night, and as I flunked and flunked and Mother began to wonder what *was* wrong, and began to blame herself, and inform me how hard she was trying, I decided to at last truly go into the fog. I'd maintain a face for others to judge me as they saw me, making sure they'd never see me, and my secrets, or my secret of secrets: my vagueness as talisman in a yearning for touch in guilt and terror, that first, rather than respond to myself responding to the actual world, and what I actually felt which was so confusing it wore me out.

I laughed and clowned around on the top of my days. My stammer got worse—it wasn't the attractive stutter other kids had. Mine was in my throat and it involved breathing, and any sentence that began with a vowel caused my throat to constrict in a violence that almost made me vomit. I invented alternatives, and when called upon to read from a textbook, and my eye fell on the vowel at the beginning, my body temperature fired, my face flushed, I dripped sweat and as I froze on my feet by my desk, I clenched the book fearing it would fly from my hands or drop with a clatter on the floor, and as the teacher faced me waiting, tense as a violin note about to explode, I lowered my head and suffered as the other kids watched as I stood hunched, crimson and gasping, until I learned to insert a word beginning with a consonant, as the bridge to the one that began with a vowel, so *Well* was my invented beginning of the text, and when called to read the text only, I could, because once I got going I was okay.
The nightmare was at the beginning.

The worst vowel of all was I, as In '76 the sky was red, and bad King George couldn't sleep in his bed, and in the face of it I lied in any possible way to avoid the hell of trying to say it, the least of which was to readily admit I hadn't done my homework, so didn't know what I was reading, a short-lived respite, as when I turned to the page, and the opening word began with an I, I went into a doubled anxiety, as in a realization of self-betrayal, it was a different I whom I'd double-crossed, as well as the other, which meant that fog could betray.

It was in that way that I learned that the world would go on without me, as Red, Gene, and Mac and all the others advanced in school, while I stayed behind.

The morning of the day I was confirmed I met the girl from across the street in our garage and as there was no place to do it, the dirt floor was a mess, we decided on the wheelbarrow, so she took off her panties, sat in the wheelbarrow, pulled up her dress and with the tip of my dick I touched her there and got both of us gooey. She smelled tangy, like milk, sweat, and salt. I didn't know what to do, she got out of the wheelbarrow, put on her panties and straightened her dress. I opened the garage doors, looked out, nobody was there and she went down the driveway the back way, and across the street home.

I closed the garage doors as she disappeared around the other side of the nextdoor neighbors' house, and Mother called out I should come in quickly and get dressed for church. That afternoon.

Bishop Scarlett put his hands on my head as I knelt at the altar rail before him, and as he gave benediction I ate the Body and Blood and loved the sensation of his hands, and their Grace, on my temples, and I felt guilt, too, because of what had happened in the garage, and the wheelbarrow, and suddenly I felt my head get sweaty, and hoped he wouldn't feel it, her folks were Catholics and about as funny as Germany, boy if she told! and feeling myself as two in two places—the garage and the Bishop's hands, I yet felt— it was me! holding my head in my hands! *And* that it was okay! I looked up at him—a glance, really, and smiled. He was a wonderful man, with the warmest smile I ever saw, and I was so grateful I made a couple of resolutions.

On the way to school we went over a hill, and coming home afterwards I so often stood on top of the hill to look down into the heart of my hometown. The air from the busy lives of people in their shops and stores and banks and businesses mixed with people shopping seemed to rise and form a vertical shimmer, and following it up I gazed into what seemed the heart of the sky, feeling myself in it.

I had gazed along stretches of farmlands and along highways, and out along the Atlantic Ocean, feeling contact with vast space, and its inner tremble.

I walked down the hill into town with my largely unopened textbooks under my arm, with a lot of other kids going my way. Kirkwood Road was a stream. I was smoking a cigarette, and as I approached the center of town I saw a big army truck coming towards me, and then another, in fact a convoy, bumping over the tracks just before passing Howell's Hardware, heading south, and as I walked north passing the newspaper—*The Kirkwood Messenger*—one of the trucks passed me, and I turned to see its cargo, which was also in all the other trucks in the convoy too, while on the sidewalk in front of me, other kids waved—to grinning, unshaven, weary middle-aged Nazi prisoners-of-war, who waved back to us, and as I walked home after the motor-column had passed, I wondered why they had waved! And grinned to us! Shouldn't they be serious? and it was odd, but they seemed pleased, because, obviously, they were out of the fighting, and though they were the losers, the Americans would take care of them and I felt a sort of patriotic tingle! But then, they were obviously angry. Well, *I* certainly was a good American! And a lot of kids had waved. Anyway some of the Nazis had seemed amused.

I was reading *Air Trails,* and admiring that bright orange Beechcraft seaplane, as I lay on the bed by the window. It was around nine p.m., and Mouse was working on his camera, at his desk. He nodded, put a Wings cigarette in the ashtray and exhaled, laughing.

"Yeah," he breathed. "You take the cake."

The Kirkwood Messenger newspaper office and printing plant was two blocks across the tracks on the same (west) side of Kirkwood Road, a block south from Howell's Hardware.

One of Mother's many duties was getting the Grace Church *Parish Messenger,* a weekly newsletter in pamphlet form, printed and mailed out. It was printed at *The Messenger,* but we did the collating and folding, and after running them through the addressograph, we put stamps on and mailed them. My sister, and once in a while some of the kids, helped, too, but mostly it was myself and Mother.

Fee, Mother said, from behind her desk in the parish office, would you run down to *The Messenger* and get the proofs?

It was, as the process of printing interested me, an attractive errand. I walked up to Adams, turned right and headed west to Kirkwood Road, which I crossed, turned left and walked south across the tracks where I passed Howell's Hardware, City Hall, crossed Monroe, and after passing a store on the corner that was going broke, I went next door, up two steps and into the front office of the newspaper into that great *smell* and racket of presses, told Miss (Nancy) Meyer—the editor—that I was Mrs. Dawson's son and I'm here to get the proofs for—

I know, Fee, she smiled: just a second, I'll see if Lee's got 'em.

She rose from her littered desk, went in back, and a few minutes later, came out and handed the folded sheets to me.

"How's your mother?"

Fine, Miss Meyer, I said.

"Tell her we said hello."

I grinned, said sure, and headed back to the parish house.

The owner of the paper was (David) Lee Jones. He had three sons: Dave (II), Herb, and Tom who had just been born. Wife, Margaret.

I was in seventh grade when Mother and Mr. Jones got together and decided I should work down at the paper on Saturdays. Lee Jones's All Day Saturday's Printer's Devil to sweep and clean the place up for two bits, which bought a lot of things, a 10¢ War Stamp, ten different kinds of candy a penny each and two big jelly doughnuts for a nickel.

My little printer's devil, Mother said, which I liked. The devil after printer beckoned like a dare to me, and I showed up that first Saturday at ten, when I was supposed to, and every Saturday morning thereafter at ten fifteen and ten thirty, sneaking in, or trying to, behind Mr. Jones's back while he sat at the linotype machine, which was just this side of the door to the front office, so he always saw me, and I had to stop as he tilted back in the wooden chair, turned, and looked at me.

'Better late than never,' eh?

I made a crooked smile.

He made a thin smile, and went back to work, shaking his head:

Well, I don't know. I just don't know. Go on, get your broom and go to work.

He had a *great* Missouri accent.

I began to sweep up. To me, the place was big, and crowded, dominated by the large flatbed press in the back, off of which the paper was run. There were a couple of smaller presses, and one speed press, stone top tables, and racks and racks of type.... The smell was beautiful, but the toilet in the back stank beyond belief.

The other paper in town, *The Advertiser*, was owned and run by a man who Mother said was an alcoholic, and who occasionally visited *The Messenger*. Came in, pulled up a chair, and sat by Mr. Jones at the linotype, and said,

Hiya Lee, how's things?

Mr Jones nodded, finished setting up the paragraph, and turned to him.

All right. How about you?

I didn't hang around to listen, though I wanted to, but if Mr. Jones'd caught me, he'd start yelling, and I'm telling you he had a voice.

So, I swept up and collected dirt, threw it in the empty drum in back and began sweeping again, stopping as often as possible to see what everyone was doing. Dave and Herb worked at the paper for sure, and I watched Dave set type and lock it up while I asked questions, until he said (we became fast friends),

Watch out, Fee, here comes Father.

I began sweeping again, and Mr. Jones walked by, stopped, looked at me, laughed, shook his head, and walked away, saying,

I don't know about you, Fee. I tell you, I wonder, and I wonder, but I just don't know.

I swept around Dave, and around the small speed press and the job presses, collected and emptied trash and swept around the bins and racks of cubbyholed wooden trays of type, shelves of paper, and I swept around the paper cutter, trying to keep out of everybody's way, and occasionally going back to take a pee—that bathroom! The stink of piss, shit, pulp paper, dampness, printer's ink, and Lava soap was glued to the air, in every corner, on every surface, floor, walls, door, sink, grease, grime, and dust on crumpled paper everywhere. The toilet bowl was stained black, irrevocably: how did it get that way? Nobody seemed to know or care, and as I had to pass the bathroom to empty the dustpan into the big drum by the back door, I often heard piss stream amid deep rumbling farts, plopping shit and the sounds of grunting men in the sharp sweet tang of cigarette smoke, as somebody sang out,

Oh gimmie land, rrrr um. G-blop, lots of land
Under starry skies above, somebody up front whistled.
Don't, I sang, fence me in.
Inaudible chuckle.

I swept up the aisle toward the linotype where Mr. Jones was at work, the light above the keyboard bright on the copy, fingers flickering across the keyboard, or occasionally adjusting the brass keys, and the windowed tin separators, his head, face and eyes, glasses down on the end of his nose, intent on his work—hat back on his head, and his thin light brown hair down on the side, cigarette dangling from his lips, hard to sweep because of the figure of him, with his sport coat open, white shirt open at the collar, and his diagonally striped tie loosened, appeared as a vision of something of mine to go into print the way he set it in type before me.

Work. Work. Work.

All stray metal lying on the thick tin apron nailed to the floor beneath the linotype machine—any metal chunk, hunk, slug, or scrap, including lead dust, curlicues, and splinters, on the apron by his left foot, went into the melter, which was set in below, on the lower left down from the keyboard. I swept the scraps and bits up, carefully separated dirt from the metal, and dropped the lead scraps into the melter. He went on working. I picked up a neat handful of warm slugs, and seeing the clean type, it looked okay to me, upside down and backwards (it and me), I looked at it, couldn't read it, it looked okay, I—hesitated, and waited until he figured out I was there, and as he glanced at me impatiently above his glasses, he wore bifocals, I held it out, and asked—stammered—should I?

Yes, God *dammit* Fee, I told you, if you see it there—

I mumbled okay okay and carefully dropped it in the melter, swept under the chair and around him and went back, emptied the dust pan, returned, and began toward the front office, which was considerably smaller, but as he had repeatedly told me to wash the front windows and the glass door, and I'd kept putting if off by staying busy in back, I could hear his voice telling me to clean those God damned windows Fee, and nobody said Fee like he did, he used it like punctuation Fee God dammit Fee clean those God damned windows period. And when I came in late one Saturday, he got so hot he cussed words I can't remember, spun around on the chair and pointed an ink-stained finger at me,

You come in late next week, you're going home so fast you won't know whether to shit or chase butterflies: get the *hell* to work! I want that door and those GOD damned windows WASHED!

Okay, I sighed, I won't be late anymore and I'll wash the door, and windows, which I did, and while cleaning up in back I heard the front door jingle familiarly, but then a crash, and—

That God *damned* Fee, why that son of a bitch *did* it! he yelled, turning to Nancy Meyer, and adding with an angry laugh, I nearly walked through the *#%!¿-door! Why in hell didn't you tell me? In so doing.

I'd made a step into a special future.

After a while as I had learned to read upside down and backwards, though not very well, and was doing things besides sweeping—stapling, counting, folding, collating —even on occasional afternoons after school—yet while sweeping I'd find blocks of set slugs on the apron under the linotype that looked so good I had to read it to make sure, and when in real doubt I asked Dave, who read it, and said, No, toss it out, I remember Father made changes. Or, on extremely rare occasions, Dave said,

You'd better ask Father.

So, with a heavy heart I approached Mr. Jones, and holding out the block of set slugs, I closed my eyes and stammered I was uncertain about this, I asked Dave, I read it, I mean, and he—he said to ask you.

Mr. Jones sat back, pushed his hat to the side of his head, and asked,

He did, did he? Where'd you find it?

O-On the apron, under the melter, Mr. Jones.

Well, what in hell have I said?

Okay, I nodded. I won't do it again, I promise, and like the glass door incident, I made another little step as he had set up the weekly editorial and had been interrupted by a salesman, so he put it on the apron underneath the melter and rose to greet the fellow in the front office as I came sweeping along, saw the block of set slugs, and threw 'em in the melter.

Well.

After the dust and the language settled down, Mr. Jones began setting the editorial again. He grinned, scratched his head, and apologized to me, chuckling to himself.

Well Fee that makes me one big horse's ass, don't it, and you don't have to be afraid to know it, because I know that's what you're thinking, so if you're ever in doubt again, ask me. I'll put up with it. And I'll damned sure never do it again.

Laughing to himself. I went on working.

Well, he said, I got what I God damned well deserved.

At school one day, Dave saw me in the corridor on my way to study hall, and asked if I could come down to the office right after school, he needed help on a rush job. I said sure, eagerly, and he added, with a grin,

"You'll get a little more than two bits."

When I showed up he was waiting for me, and we went in the back as he explained the job would be done on the big flatbed press. He'd feed, and I'd be at the other end to receive and make sure the sheets of paper didn't stack crookedly, or jam.

The job was for a paper out in the county. Something had gone wrong, and Mr. Jones had agreed to do it. It had to be done that evening for the morning pickup.

The sheets of paper were as large as those *The Messenger* was printed on, which was the same size (though not so many pages) as the *The Post-Dispatch,* and I stood on the metal platform at the end watching Dave feed, and the sheets came off the roller sliding onto a row of long tines which rose and swept up, gracefully over and down in a slow, gentle slap, to land before me. I kept each sheet in line on the stack, and as the machine stopped instantly, no matter at what stage of the process it was, Dave, as I glanced at him, always met my eyes, and I realized he was watching me as well as the press and the sheets of paper, small wonder, and in the inevitable jams he stopped the machine, and cleared it, as he was closer, often without my help, though often with it. So the work went. I loved it. Around eight o'clock we were through.

I had telephoned Mother and told her where I was, and as Dave and I carried the big stack of pages to the large table by the press, he said the girls were coming in early to collate and fold, so we washed up and left. Dave locked the front door and we began walking home along Kirkwood Road.

He opened his wallet, took out a ten-dollar bill, and gave it to me:

Father asked me to give you this.

He laughed, knowing, at fourteen (our age), I'd never had ten dollars to call my own in my life. I folded it, and put it in my wallet, and as we walked I felt my wallet burn, and my two-for-a-nickel jelly doughnut and penny candy imagination ran down the street in front of me, as in a dream we passed City Hall, and Howell's Hardware, crossed the tracks, Argonne Drive, and went through the Kirkwood shopping section, crossed Adams, and at Washington we stopped. We talked a little, then waved so long.

See you tomorrow in school! I cried, in twilight.

Thanks a lot, Fee!

Later *The Messenger* moved to two new locations, and finally ended up on West Argonne Drive between the fire department and the undertaker, Ferd Bopp (rhyme with pope), and myself as well as other kids in town said it BOP!

Mr. Meechum was at least ninety, and stood tall, straight, skinny as a beanpole, day in and day out appeared dressed in black: plus top hat, and cane, face gaunt and eyes steady: walking slowly. Formal. Proud as a prince, but poor as a pauper.

One of the firemen spotted him heading west on Argonne.

Lookout Meechum! Ferd's gonna think yer one of *HIS!*

Mr. Jones's wife Margaret was a small woman. I really liked her. It was because I worked at the paper that I became friendly with them as a family, and especially with Dave and Herb, and many nights I stayed over, in their big house, on the second story long-windowed porch in the back which overlooked the yard. Their house was really huge, with a big yard, and trees. In darkness, from our bunks, we talked, and in suspense, Dave, just like his father, would say,

Fee, if a blue stone fell into the Red Sea, what would happen?

And I racked my brains, in color combinations, word puns, and everything in full thrill never guessing it would get wet.

They had a big kitchen, and a wonderful maid. Breakfasts were so much fun, and so good, with such warm people.

One Saturday I saw a stranger talking to Mr. Jones, when Mother came in with some additional copy for the *Parish Messenger,* and seeing the other man, she changed and I was—tense, and frightened, instantly.

They greeted her, and with a shock I saw the strange man's fly was unbuttoned.

Mr. Jones rose from his swivel chair, and took Mother up front, asking her how she was, and as she said Just fine, Lee, we want to publish something a little different this week, and she wanted to talk with him about it, otherwise she wouldn't have disturbed him—

But the stranger had watched Mother walk out, he had run his eyes up and down her figure, and had gotten a set hard look on his face, especially in his eyes, and after a while I heard the door jingle shut, Mr. Jones came back, and looked at me.

Get to work, he said. You can't be standin' around gawkin' all day.

He sat down in the chair, and began setting type, as the other man, standing, looked down at him, and as I swept my way to the back, I heard Mr. Jones say, to the man,

What's this I hear about Kroger's?

Mr. Jones? I asked, after the man had gone, can I ask you something, I mean—

He tilted his head down, and looked at me above his bifocals, and smiled.

"Fee," he said. "It takes all kinds of horses to make a race."

We smiled together, and a couple of hours later, when I got it, I laughed, and when I told Mother, we shared it, and she said, with a long look in her eye, Lee's a wonderful man.

Then she added, softly,

There aren't many men like Lee Jones.

I had seen the three older guys hanging around the gate in the fence along Kirkwood Road, having a smoke. Before and after school. The smallest of them was a couple of inches taller than me, and the next guy was a couple of inches taller than him, but the tallest and biggest guy's name was Brooks, and he was a hero on the football team. They were all Juniors, and one day after I had finished my lip-reading class, and was on my way back to study hall, but stopped in the boys' room for a quick smoke, I was astonished to see the three of them there, in the bathroom too, by the wall near the open window, and their faces careful. But when they saw it was me, it was not necessarily okay, but it was better than Hendricks, the principal, who was noted for checking the toilets.

I sniffed the air, grinned, smiled rather shyly, and said, me—

Me too!

They laughed, threw their cigarettes in a toilet, flushed it, and left. I ducked into the last cubicle, closed the door, had a fast smoke, flushed it down, and after closing the window, I left too, chewing gum. Double my pleasure. After school that day I followed them, caught up with them and stood around and had a smoke with 'em, listening until I got their nicknames. I told them my name, and as they had known my sister—she had graduated the year before (1943), then suddenly they had heard of me because of the streetcar accident, as well as being the little brother, so as they were friendly, I began making sure to see them after school, but hurt when they got in Hoot's two-tone light gray and blue torpedo-backed Buick coupe and left, but happy to have been with them for that brief moment, and in fact I began to tag after them. They didn't seem to object, I made 'em laugh showing off and telling stories about Uncle Mouse, Uncle Mousie, Brooks called him, How's Uncle Mousie? which made me laugh, and get excited, trembling and stammering, disliking that *ie* on the end. Brooks had an obvious lisp on consonants, and thus called me Thee, and as I had my bad stammer on vowels, our dialogues were funny, and it was good his name began with a B.

Though I never went out with them (I wanted to!), I in a way became their after-school mascot.

Gene and Mac and I went to the junior high dances, not to dance—not for me anyway (they did), it terrified me, although it hurt not to, because the girls were so beautiful, I mostly watched. Mac and Gene danced, and I envied them, yet was irritated because they looked so foolish, but they didn't look foolish at all. If I were out there, *I* would, so I stayed near the wall and drank Cokes and watched, in an angry dismay, knowing I was too self-conscious and afraid and I wished they'd quit dancing and come and be with me. And anyway, we snuck into the senior high dances where everybody was always bigger, older, taller, better dressed, the guys were way more handsome, more cool than I who merely decorated the wall, trying to put on a face to fit the wall, anxious flower that I was, while I watched the girls move, in that dark gym, while the band played and the world belonged to the Seniors in something like a deep and unreachable dark blue flash just over the rim of midnight. The whites of the girls' eyes gleamed, teeth cracked titanium in grins to break hearts, and breath came fast, They're Either Too Young Or Too Old and I was too frightened, as their bodies spun and skirts swirled, with tall blue-white guys in the sharp dark suits whirling in the glittering jitterbug, while the band played songs by Tommy Dorsey and Harry James. My eyes drilled into the eyes of her delighted laughter and outcry, quick intake of breath, parted lips, rustling skirt, and his face, smiling at the cut-in with the dark looks, the long looks, the shy looks, and the look of actors and actresses in mask. Parents, teachers, principal and his assistant standing by, in their power, and once in a while *he* danced with *her,* the girls were delighted, and the tough guys from Valley Park watched with narrowed eyes, but the guys and girls in love couldn't care less, dancing in the slow fox-trot, her head on his shoulder, fair hair tumbling as his white cheek touched hers. I saw his scalp through his crew cut, above his white collar and dark green jacket, and I was almost helpless. I saw it, liked it, and wanted it, as the way to do it was to love it like not caring, but to love it so much that a little overflowed, and like Artie and Nancy, or Red and Ellie, everybody could see love and to the lovers it didn't matter at all.

But when the line began to run out, and the suspense began to get tensile, "Star Dust" came on to cries and pleas, dreamers and lovers, the last dance was the last dance forever, which I admired, though jealous and angry, but that it meant so much was hardly a secret, and as Gene and Mac and I walked home afterwards, from the top of the hill I looked down into the bright street-lit heart of Kirkwood at night, its lights glowing warmly, quietly, quietly.

He felt her in his heart.

I had seen Brooks, Hoot, and Earl at the dance, though, —a heartleap!—and they'd smiled and waved. They each had dates, and the six of them walked in together, and of course I wouldn't be jealous of them because they were the big guys and it was—I mean it was right.

But as we walked down the hill and into town, and looked into store windows, and particularly at the movie stills outside the Osage Theatre, I felt sad, and puzzled, in my quiet town, and standing on the empty well-lighted sidewalk I yearned for the future in an unbearable way.

Seen dancing with a girl. I'd been seen in school, at home, on the street and the ballfield, and everybody—who could ignore me?—reacted to my showing off, angel's face with wings in the choir at church, but underneath, where I lived, was where I wanted to be with her, in a different way. Be with the girl, and in a way, around and in her, as she would be with me, and how could I lose myself with her in a public place?

How could I lose myself when the self and I were all involved with me? Maybe that's where the fog came from. I don't think so—I dunno. Anyway, I could, could I?, get lost there. Yes no. I couldn't figure it out. When I was with girls I wanted to be lost, alone with her, and hoped she would with me too, but how do you *be* with a girl? and nobody must see especially Mother, because it was me, getting lost, in each other's arms as us, hopefully for me.

Brooks said: *Hoot.* The Earl said it softly, Hoot. Hoot made a mellow smile as he joined them. Then I was there. Hi, Hoot! and saw his car across the street. Him.

The most dapper of the three, in lightweight yellow plaid sports jacket, pink shirt, and tapered powder blue slacks always creased and oxblood loafers always shined. The pennies too. The argyle socks he wore were of a conservative pattern and color, and matched anything. His leather belt was pencil-thin through the long belt-loops and held his pants snug against his flat stomach. His shirt was open at the collar, and underneath the reversed tee shirt made a horizontal white glint against his throat, and as his shoulders were narrow, which he knew, he was, in fact, thin to a point of being skinny, like his belts, and the sports jackets he wore were as neat and crisp as anything else he put on him, but could, if anyone looked close, seem to hang on him.

His face V-tapered, like his short sharp narrow-nostrilled nose. His lips were thin, and his thin curly hair was light brown, and worn in a wave. He wore big round tortoise shell glasses, which is how he got his nickname.

Hoot knew what he wanted.

He also knew what was inevitable, and what the three of them seemed to be planning was how to get what they wanted, which was what every other guy wanted, her, but from an inside selection rather than the outside settlement. When they got their heads together they almost buzzed.

The Earl was like Hoot, just as meticulous, but whereas Hoot was conspicuously dapper, Earl, in his varieties of clothes, was neatly inclined to steady combinations without sports jackets. I could walk like Earl. He took short steps and swung his shoulders, and held his head and his lips pressed in a line like an expectant shortstop, saying things like Let's do it, you do it, I'll watch, as Brooks and Hoot laughed, Brooks more uncontrollably than Hoot. Brooks's father was a laborer, and as he (Brooks) was one of several kids, he didn't have much money. Not like Hoot, who I believe had a job. Hoot also had a sister who in fact resembled him closely, yet was more outgoing and, I thought, much smarter. Though I didn't know her at all. I did a terrific drawing of Hoot.

Is all they did was talk about girls. And sports.

It was Sammy Gardner, or at least Sammy Gardner was the first softball pitcher I ever saw, to use the windmill delivery, and around 1940 or 1941, it was really something. But by the end of the season a couple of teams had pitchers faster and with better stuff, and more control than Sammy. But Sammy was good, and held his own no matter. The next year everybody pitched windmill.

Brooks had a bad reputation because he drank and got into fights, which his scarred and swarthy face showed, so he was identified with an element in Kirkwood most folks regarded as belonging to Valley Park, but it never bothered me, and I was at that football game when Brooks got the ball, ran with it around the right end, raised his arm to pass as the opposing half of the left end hit him all together, as he yet staggered forward, keeping his arm raised high with players hanging on his neck, hips, shoulders, and back, spotting his receiver in the open Brooks shifted under the weight, and while the Kirkwood stands went crazy, he threw an ankle-high windmill pitch on a line into the receiver's hands for a solid first down, and afterwards, in complete frenzy, Brooks was hardly able to talk, or stand, in his laughter, at his Submarine Pass. Hoot, the Earl—and I —loved it. Well he had a few beers and some whiskey once in a while, so what. Got drunk, yes. Big deal.

Earl's grin. Hoot's eyes and big leer. They stood with

Brooks in the mess and din and stink of the football locker room.

On the radio, a deep bass growl in an echo chamber: attenuated: beeeeeoh, and The Great Gildersleeve's old maid laugh.

That spring Brooks was pitching a close game. I was there, and with men on base, the Earl, who was catching, signaled the umpire and trotted out to talk with Brooks. MacMahon, the manager, watched. He knew those guys. Earl gave Brooks the ball, and standing close said something. Brooks's face changed, he straightfaced covered a sudden laugh, then looked angry, not daring to glance at Mac as Earl hustled back behind the plate, Brooks looked at the men on base, and when Earl went into position, Brooks looked in for the sign, got it, and went into the stretch.

YOU SON OF A BITCH YOU FUCKED ME *UP* Brooks yelled at Earl, after the game, as Earl and Hoot laughed, Man I was in a *jam* and you knew it and there was *Mac*—Oh Jesus Earl! Say a crazy thing like that.
What'd he say? Hoot asked.

Old Buttermilk Sky, I'm tellin' you why when the green lime went into the ice-filled glass, followed by Coke, and the color changed after a couple of stirs with a straw the chilled deep sweetness went down so well. Mrs. Carpenter had the best banana splits in the county, and we sat around her little restaurant listening to "Opus #1," and tapped our feet, Brooks following the rhythm with Earl, with their hands on the edge of the table as they talked about girls and I practiced my pig latin, and again got confused, beginning as always from the natural base, Eeldingfay Awsonday, and working it from there. There were kids who held whole dialogues. Not me, though. Vowels wouldn't let me.

Carpenter's was the most popular after-school hangout in town, she was really friendly, and she made the best and biggest oatmeal cookies—the best *ever*, seven cents each. The place was packed after school, and while Ella May Morse dovetailed in and out of "The House of Blue Lights" we all sat around and talked about girls, or they did, and I watched—there wasn't any dancing, not allowed—as they made plans in what I thought was the niftiest little place around, the way the sun came through the front windows, and the jukebox sparkled, as did the glassware, and the girls' eyes, to be there was something, after school, as before or after it was quiet, yet even in the quiet I heard the vivid sounds as of Kirkwood High after school, somehow brilliant, clean, and wonderful, right on Kirkwood Road, so near *The Messenger*, as traffic sped by to or from Highway 66: New York, San Francisco, and the world while American men not much older than Brooks, Hoot, and the Earl sang the same songs we were hearing on the jukebox in faraway places with strange-sounding names brutally dealing death while they took it, and the bright guys imitated Churchill's snarl, *We have chased the Nazee beast into its lair*, and each and every one of us, later that day and every day listened in a way we'd never listened before, to CBS and the most memorable journalist of all, doing his best to actualize flesh and machines merging in murder, as the radio crackled, went faint, much, no doubt, like the journalist himself, having had such a long night of talking foreign policy, and perhaps smoking imported cigars, but definitely enjoying the brandy, which is what Churchill meant, when he called, Edward, why don't you come over? I have some excellent brandy. . . .

Churchill didn't pronounce it Natzi like we did.

Oh the girls all called him—who, Brooks? Me? "Johnny Zero." Mrs. Carpenter's husband had died in an industrial accident and her son, who had gone to Kirkwood High, just as she had, had been killed in the Pacific, so the star in the window was significant, and another reason why we went there. "Three Little Fishies (and a mama fishie too)"— Ishkabibble. Luminous faces in a crowd.

Stop—

Okay.

All the blood in the Lizard's father's face had drained, cheekbones turning pink as he screamed:

FIELDING YOU ARE AN IDIOT!

AN — *IDIOT!* he added, while behind me Steve was on his hands and knees in the dirt, waiting. Me too. Except I was on my feet, and the Lizard's dad was on the other side of the fence. And what caused his outcry was, at the outset, a surprise to us all. Mr. Matthews had informed us that the tennis court would no longer be used, so we could dig it up all we wanted.

His oldest son, a Navy pilot, was missing in action. There was a star in the window.

And that was the day the Great Tank Wars began, and we were on the Sahara, under the blistering sun. Thirsty.

So with Steve's Dinky Toys, by midafternoon, the tennis court was pretty well ruined. We had trenches, antiaircraft emplacements, landing strips, gas depots, hospitals, etc., and when the Lizard's dad came home from work he almost fell over. He got out of the car, and ran to the fence, crying Boys! Boys! You're ruining the tennis court, etc., and we looked up.

What is the meaning of this? he asked, through the fence.

Go tell him, said Steve.

I rose, dusted off my knees, went to the fence, and listened to some more words, and when he paused, I reached up, put the tip of each index finger at the outside corner of each eye, and pulled up, slanting my eyes. I put a sleepy look on my face, drew my mouth down, and said,

Ah sir, if you would, so kindly, please speak a lee-tle Jah-pan-eeze, we might, perhaps, understand.

Go.

I walked across the yard between cottages to the small cool cave in the side of the mountain in which everything that would spoil was kept. It was the spookiest, creepiest, weirdest and scariest place I was ever in and when Mommy asked me to go get stuff, I—didn't want to. But I also did, it was so spooky I couldn't resist, although just a couple of minutes in there alone was enough.

I was barefoot, and in short pants. No shirt.

The door was rickety in a rough wood frame set into the earth, and we went in and out just as easily as we would a house or a cottage, except there was a way that door hung that it couldn't hang in a house. It opened easy, with a soft squeak, a little crookedly, too, but when I got it open, it hung back like it was disappointed, and then came forward and closed itself. Jess and Mommy told me not to keep holding that door open because the food inside would spoil, so we had to open the door, and quickly, so we could see what we were doing, while holding it open, step in, take what we wanted with both hands and step out before the door swung back, hung, and then closed. There wasn't any light inside, the light from the open doorway was it. Otherwise we used kitchen matches, or if somebody had to be in there a while, candles or lanterns. I opened the door slowly, because that first smell and sight of damp earth was like going into a dead man's mouth. I stepped in. Scared clear through. Barefoot. Cold, damp earth. My legs began to shake, heart pounding, as I held the door open, in my doing wrong again, holding it open by stretching out my hand, and turning, I faced, just beyond hand's reach, the crocks of milk, butter, clabber, cheese, lard, etc., and in the bright shaft of sunlight coming through behind me, I saw, on the rough cut dirt wall, which was damp with sweat, roots like hair, or bleached grass, long and dangling, glistening, and among them the insects of the under earth: brilliant centipedes of all sizes, shiny little spiders, and bugs like dots that stretched and curled, and what looked like crickets, but big, and black as freshly painted iron that crouched on the wall beside me, and over my head, I could touch 'em if I wanted, oh no, but I saw feelers fluttering and adjusting to the sunlight. I was especially scared to step on a slug and there were slugs everywhere, white and blind and slimy and cold, like a naked snail, but big, fat, and clean full of rot, mud, and other smaller insects, however well digested, that's what slugs were. What a world! I took a step forward, quickly lifted the cheesecloth with my left hand and dipped the cup into the butter with my right, as the door hesitated, and then swung shut. For a—I couldn't see and I was scared something wild boy I went through that door like a jackrabbit, and stood outside on the grass breathing hard. I looked at the closed door. Then, putting the cup of butter on the grass, I opened the door again, and looked in. The cricket had moved a little, and on the sweaty dirt wall to its left I saw a big long pale gray insect with wings, sitting beside it, in roots, feelers moving. I saw some tiny insects, too, ones I'd missed before they were so small and me so scared. They walked around, ducked into tiny holes, and peeped out. That place was crawling with life. I let the door close, and crossed to our cottage the way I had come. 1937: Daddy in New York, Mommy and me and Ca in the mountains of Pennsylvania, the summer I turned seven, in a small community called Muddy Run.

Our cottage was pretty near the creek, and the bridge
which led to the road to town, and walking that way and
after crossing the bridge and turning right, was the patch of
tiger lilies, except it was bigger than a patch, it was a whole
long and deep patch, and Mommy and I picked tiger lilies.
*We filled our arms with tiger lilies. The stems were green
and long, and the freckled orange blooms unfurled,
beautifully. Mommy wore them in her hair, the most
beautiful Mommy walked above the earth, with tiger lilies
in her snow white hair and her arms filled with tiger lilies,*
as we crossed the bridge, *my arms full of tiger lilies as
I skipped along beside her, everything in the world,* happy,
humming and following bees through the orchard, and on
the blueberry hills beyond, at the foot of the mountains, at
home forever in *tiger lilies.*

Our cheeks together, looking into their hearts.

I was walking along in the twilight, barefoot among the chickens and turkeys by the pigpen, when I felt something funny in my foot, so I sat down on the ground, and in the dim light saw and felt the nail, and began to whimper as Jess strode quickly to me, and kneeling down beside me, took a look at it.

The head of the nail stuck out about half an inch from the soft under arch. I felt nausea at the ugly dead feel, and when Jess held my foot tightly with one hand, and with the other, in one motion pulled the nail out I almost cried it was so awful. There wasn't any blood, but that nail was big, at least two inches, and as he picked me up I put my arms around his neck and put my head on his shoulder. We walked across to his cottage, he told his wife to get Mrs. Dawson, which was done, and after Jess applied peroxide, Mother and Jess and I went to Jess's truck to, as he said, get me to the doc's for the shot, and that trip was awful, and scary, and I was really glad to get back. I limped around for a couple of days after, and had to wear a bandage, a sock, and one shoe until my foot was okay, and I could go barefoot again, but more carefully for sure as I passed the pigpen.

Mommy heard a terrific clatter. She stepped outside, and saw a horse racing across the bridge, head up, wild-eyed and mane flying, with a cloud of bees after him. The horse ran into the yard in front of the cottages, and then ran crazily in circles until Jess came, quieted, and held the horse steady, and oh RATS I wasn't there. She told me later. Jess got the bees to a tree, and that tree looked like a humming bee-tree!

Mommy. Talking with Jess's wife.

Oh that boy. And those caterpillars!

I know, Jess's wife said. They like caterpillars, but he does seem over happy with 'em.

Well, he is, Mother explained. He says the ones across the valley are best.

Two women amused.

And yesterday, Mommy said, as I was doing the laundry, I went to turn his pockets, and they were filled with them. *Ugh,* awful! *Brr*—

Then she laughed, and said, you know, Fee likes snakes, too, and when we were in Florida—Clarence had a job there, last year—Fee brought me a black snake as a present. It was about four feet long, and he and his friends had it over their shoulders, like a rope, and he came up the back steps, knocked on the kitchen door, and when I opened it I couldn't believe my eyes. He said he brought me a present, and the other boys grinned and laughed and he did, too, saying it wouldn't hurt me because it was asleep, and it was, too, sound asleep on their shoulders. He likes spiders as well, and was fascinated by a dead sea turtle, used to go down to the beach and watch vultures eat it. I told him to take the black snake away and let it sleep, to put it in a shady place and not disturb it, and he did.

They're harmless creatures. Does he mind the daddy-long-leg spiders here?

Mind them? Anything but! I don't like 'em much, but what can I do?

How about his sister?

They don't bother her, either, though a little. But they

walk all over him, asleep or awake! He laughs! They seem to like *him!*

Ha ha ha!

A great wide rock overhung the creek, and it's where the women did the laundry, and washed their hair, until Jess, who thought he had seen snakes near there, pried the rock up, and there they were: a nest of copperheads. He killed 'em okay—they had been the length of his shotgun away from the women's faces and hands, and he wouldn't let me watch. I missed it all, but Jess consoled me. Nobody else saw it either, except from so far away they couldn't see anything except the gun going off. He wouldn't let *any*body near.

That valley was filled with daddy-long-legs and I loved them. They were everywhere, by the thousands, honest, so thick on the screen on the porch we could hardly see out. They wouldn't hurt anybody so we weren't scared, but they were on the table when we ate, in our beds, in the sink and on the dishes, and when I ate my oatmeal in the morning they'd come across the table, climb up my wrist, walk down along my hand and fingers to the spoon. Once one bunched up its long legs and leaned over the tip of the spoon to see what was there: milk, so it stopped to puzzle out what milk was, decided it didn't want any, so stepped over onto the island made by the oatmeal, and crossed to the opposite edge of the island, reached up to the edge of the bowl, climbed up, over and down to and across the table to the vase of tiger lilies, climbed up the side of the vase, along the stalks until it got up to the blooms, where it stopped, and stayed on top of its tiger lily world as I watched, leaned forward, and we looked at each other.

Ca and I walked up the mountain. Jess said not to but we did anyway. We knew there was a cave up there. He said not to go because of the snakes. They were thick on the mountain, which we also knew. The trees were big, and the vines and underbrush were heavy, dense and damp, lush and eerie. There was, at the outset, a path, and when we got to the end of it, the bushes and vines were almost too thick.

We kept saying we oughta go back, but holding hands we went on, and after an hour or so, we saw it: above a rock slide, and in a clearing between trees, under an overhang of rocks. The cave went back about six or eight feet, like a slash into the mountain, and we climbed up the rock face, and then on our stomachs, breathing heavy, peered in.

It was shaded, and warm and damp. We saw leaves, and sticks, boy that place *felt* snake, and we didn't see a one. We looked at each other: Shall we go in? We wanted to, go in, turn around and look out, down into the valley, which is what caves were for, but we didn't 'cause that cave was snake-heaven, it was what resting snakes feel of, it was all snake-heat, and we felt snake eyes on us, their miniature hot breath and the sparkle on the tips of fangs in a smell of blood. There wasn't a sound, except of the wind in the leaves, and the heavy silent sound of mountain power, and as both of us were getting the jitters, we turned from the lip of the cave, and slid and crawled back down the rocks to the grass and into the bushes and vines again, where we continued back down to the cottages.

But we came out in a different place than where we had begun, and for a second were lost. Then we saw the door to the cool storage cave, and knew where we were.

Don't tell anybody.

We didn't, either.

About a hundred and fifty yards above the bridge the creek came down around a bend and appeared at the foot of a high bank, on top of which stood an ancient maple tree in the midst of willows. The trunk of the maple was crooked, and bent in such a way that it gave, along with the willows, shade to a deep, clear-water pool beneath. We swam there. All of us. I couldn't dive but my sister could, and she dove off the bank into the wonderful cool dark water. We swam there at least once a day, when it didn't rain, and it was great to lie on the grass across from the tree, and watch her, or Mom or Jess's children. The oldest boy's name was Adam, and he and Ca were friends. We all played together. Once when we had gathered leaves I rode back on top of the heap in the wheelbarrow. I wore my wide-brimmed straw hat that day, and my bib-overalls. When Aunty Mil visited, she took some pictures, and after she had gone back to Kirkwood, she mailed them to us. The one of me in the wheelbarrow made it all look small but it was all right, nice was the word, also cute, Mommy was thrilled as was Ca, and Mommy said All right, you just wait.

Adam was Ca's age, so he was five years older'n me too. They had a lot of fun together. I loved the swimming hole, even though I couldn't swim. I paddled around the edges, quiet as a fish so I could sneak up on frogs and catch 'em nappin'. We'd look at each other, and often, so fast SNAP they'd leap—right over my SHOULDER *splash!* into the water.

My spot, across from the big tree and the willows on the high bank, was a grassy place that turned into mud and sloped into the water, so when I got all wet and had splashed the mud until it was slick I slid in the water that

way. I liked it I loved it I *loved* it, belly first, half fish, back
into the water.

I liked to watch the insects around the water hole too,
which I did without fail, just as I watched frogs, and my
favorite insects were water spiders and dragon flies.
Katydids, too. I watched and watched, and watched, and I
could figure out the water spiders, but never the dragon
flies. Or walking sticks, either.

I was sliding around in the mud one morning, my sister
and Adam were swimming and splashing each other, and he
was laughing, there wasn't any point for me to watch, until I
heard her yell at him to stop and he didn't so she yelled
louder and he didn't and when she yelled it again in a
different sound I heard she was scared! I turned and saw he
had his hands on her throat, and was pushing her under.
They were face to face and treading water. I saw her hand
flash up out of the water to hit him, and he laughed and put
his face close to hers and I saw her turn her head away, put
her hand on his shoulder and push.

About five feet out in the water beyond me the slope
took a sharp underwater drop, and I got up and ran in to
stop him, yelling at him to leave her alone, my eyes wide
open green and white as I went under, screaming, the water
flooding my mouth, nose, and throat as I was being carried
out, still crying and kicking at him, good to get my hands on
him I hit and kicked him as hard as I could, but they were
both telling me it was okay, Adam didn't mean anything,
she said, he wasn't trying to drown me, or hurt me, she
said, and as I sat on the grass and choked, sniffled,
sneezed, coughed, and wept, and she sat down beside me
and though her eyes were blurred too, probably 'cause
mine were, it did seem, though, that hers were too, and
for a while I didn't say anything and she let me cry until
I had to stop. She wiped my face with her hanky, I got up
and the three of us walked back to the cottage, he saying he

was sorry, and I was too but I was still angry 'cause she's my sister. Then—

I saw something that almost knocked me over! A great *big* dump truck drove across the bridge! Jess guided the driver, everybody anxious about the bridge giving, and it came across okay, the wheels just barely making it, and it drove across the large yard under the trees toward the foot of the mountain, me running after.

A few men were there. Two men got out of the truck with shovels, and Jess went and got some more shovels, passed them around, and where the mountain had slid, they began to dig, and throw the dirt up into the truck!

"Where's *my* shovel!" I cried, and they laughed. Well, I want to help, I said, looking at the lowered tailgate, and the dirt heaping up, with more on the way.

"I know you do," Jess said, but this is men's work. Those shovels are bigger than you are.

Mommy appeared, and I knew what she'd say but I asked her anyway and she sighed I'd only be in the way. "I know, Fee, but this is *heavy* work, and—"

Aw gee.

One of the men jumped up onto the back of the truck, and began shoveling dirt towards the front, and a couple of them looked at her, and at me. Downcast. Isn't *fair*.

I know it isn't, she said, and took my hand to lead me away but no, *not* take my hand, *not* lead me away.

I saw her looking at Jess and him looking at her, and then he said,

Look, this is a big sweaty job nobody likes, and we'll be at it all day, and most likely tomorrow. If it rains this dirt'll be swept clear across to the cottages, so we've got to get it out, and we need all the help we can get.

The other men laughed at him, as he grinned. Why did they laugh? Jess said, to me,

I have to go into town this afternoon. I'll get a shovel your size.

Mommy smiled, and I took a breath, pointed to a long-handled shovel that had a smoothly curved, beautiful steel blade, and said I want a shovel like that. Jess nodded, and one of the men handed it to me and well it was so, I mean I pushed it in the soft dirt like they did only it didn't go in like they did it, my hands slid up on the handle, the blade suddenly turned, and the handle rapped me on my lip, and in the sting I stepped back with tears in my eyes and my hand on my mouth as the men nodded. Hang around and watch, and be careful or you'll get more of the same, one of the men grinned, as the others nodded. Jess'll have you a shovel this afternoon.

I did, I watched them, and could hardly eat lunch I was so excited. Those men were so BIG, and that *truck!* The *wheels* were bigger'n *me!* I had gone to the front wheel, the truck had backed in, and I put my hand on the high wall of the tire, and felt the warm breath of the machine under the fender, and the warm hard rubber wall of the tire, and the heavy tread, and I smelled oil! And a sweet smell of gasoline on the green valley air—I stepped back, wide-eyed.

After lunch I saw Jess drive across the bridge into town, and Mother made me lie down, just for a little, which I did. Out my window I could see the men, sitting near the truck, eating sandwiches and drinking coffee under the trees. The sky was cloudy, but shafts of sunlight poured through the dark green shade where the men were, in bright yellow-green patches, as they talked, in the distance across the big yard.

I rested, heart wild, while Mommy and Ca played checkers.

Jess came back.

He had a package which he unwrapped on the front step, and gave it to me. A shovel my size, with a red wooden handle in the shape of a T, and an orange painted blade.

"Okay," he said: "let's go," and I walked along beside him to where the men and the truck were. They hadn't gotten very far, for, I noticed, there was only a small crescent in the pile. Jess pointed to a spot to the right of the crescent, on the edge of it, and told me to shovel dirt over to where one of the men could scoop it up, and when they began to work, I did too, and I—holy *smoke* that was hard work! I tried not to get in their way, but one of the men clipped my shoe with his shovel (I had to put *shoes* on), I didn't say anything and backed away, but Jess had seen it, and I saw the man and Jess exchange glances, and Jess said, to me, that this was an important job, it *had* to be done, and fast. I'd better stay out of the way. When the hardest part was over I could help clean up, they'd appreciate that more than anything, and the men agreed. I knew what he meant, I thought about it and nodded yes, that was true, so I went a little ways off and sat down under a tree, had an apple, and watched them. They sure worked hard, and that night later it was almost done, they were dripping sweat, cursing, and laughing.

I'd had supper by then, and had wandered over to see how they were doing. Jess was looking up at the night sky, which was dark, with low swiftly moving clouds. The wind came down the valley, damp and warm, and later, when I went to bed, after having watched them work by lantern light, I fell asleep, and slept as sound and as deep as a snake.

The next day I was up early, out of the cottage and across the yard. The truck was gone, and so was the dirt. Just before breakfast it had begun to rain, and later that afternoon, when it was still coming down, not hard, but steady, Jess came over and he and Mommy laughed when he said the rain's come and cleaned up for Fee. I grinned myself, I was pretty stiff, and sore, too, and only disappointed that I hadn't seen that dump truck full of dirt cross the bridge, on which Jess and the men had put heavy timbers, and watched, fearfully, as the truck rolled across.

He gave me a little bucket, and most every morning said Go get some apples, the pigs are hungry.

So I walked down the road, swinging my bucket.

The trees, right on the floor of the valley, made a natural orchard. They were small and stunted, but the apples were big and I picked them carefully, although the grass and the leaves under the trees were full of them, but mostly rotten, so I reached up, pulled the branch down, and picked apples, smelling their warm sweetness. They were spotted and pitted, kind of freckled, and hard and once in a while I ate one *um* they were good.

When my bucket was full I lay on my back in the tall grass with my arms outflung, and I watched the tops of grass blades bend in the breeze before my eyes. Refractions twinkled and blurred as blade tips touched and drifted apart. I watched bees race through the currents on the soft valley wind. I have always loved bees, and perhaps I am a bee. Little spiders floated by, windblown, on their delicate webs. I perceived the distance from my eyes to the tips of grass blades, and from there to the sailing spiders and racing bees—and gnats and flies, and birds, over the daisies and big country dandelions between mountain walls, clear down the valley.

We walked along the road, up and around turns finding arrowheads and the strangest flowers, scarlet in moss in the rocks on road banks. We cut across fields of tall grass and prickly bushes until we got to blueberry hill, where Ca and I picked blueberries, and when we got home our buckets were full, and my hands, lips, and cheeks were stained blue, from blueberries, so warm, so sweet and juicy *wonderful blueberries*.

The deep blue Pennsylvania sky arced toward the horizon, as ideas under the sun like clouds, moved along on gentle zephyrs above the directing hilltop angles of ourselves, who cast brief and complicated shadows in blueberries, from mica, and cadmium yellow, under that vast and inexplicably long blue curve above, vertical from our highest hill.

Bam.

Blairsville, Pa.

I woke fast, in an outcry—

LINDY!

Leaped out of bed, put on the socks I wore yesterday
and my sneaks, short pants, tee shirt and ran into the
kitchen—nobody there. Alone!

It wasn't all that early, either, I liked to sleep late, so it
meant Mommy had gone shopping and my sister had hum
gone wherever girls went when they went out.

I filled a bowl with cornflakes, and seeing some bananas
on the table, which were a little green, and not such a light
green either, I peeled one and sliced crisp discs on top of
the cereal and I opened the ice box, took out the milk and
smelled it like anybody from six to sixty did, in 1936, and
it smelled just a *little* sour.

It was, in fact, but not that much, but it was also ice
cold, and it looked so white and fresh I filled the bowl to the
brim, and sprinkling a teaspoon or two of sugar over it, I ate
it all right down, the bananas crunched and the milk tasted
good, cold, but kinda funny I admit, but with cornflakes
and sugar, well I put the empty bowl and spoon in the sink
and ran out the side door onto the top step.

Our kitchen was in the back of the house and we lived
on the second floor, there was a stairway that ran down the
side of the house outside, so I raced down the stairs and
across the lot to Lindy's house. I jumped up his porch steps
passing the big green swing, his front door was open and I
ran in and yelled up the stairs to the second floor, loud so
he could hear—

LINDY!

LET'S PLAY! (I waited.)

LINDY!

I put my hand on the newel post and looked anxiously up the stairs, hearing his mother say his name and then his hurrying feet on the ceiling. He came bounding down the stairs with his leather Lindy hat on, and we laughed and shouted, and I went in the kitchen with him as he drank some canned orange juice, had an apple, my stomach was feeling a little okay strange and after he had a slice of bread with stirred peanut butter and a glass of milk, we went out onto his front porch and sat on the swing, and got it going.

When the swing was *really* going we were almost to the rail of the porch, just beyond which were big bushes, which was France, and we were The Spirit of Saint Louis.

Look! cried Lindy, I see fisher-boats!

There they are, I said, urgently, pointing down, out of the plane's window, Let's dip down and say hello!

Okay! The plane dipped to the left, and down low over the Atlantic, and the boats.

We waved to the French fishermen, and they waved back. We waved again and told them who we were, and they waved up to us wishing us good luck. We waved again, and they did too, and then after waving again, and they too, we gained altitude and headed for land.

It isn't far away!

Lindy spoke into the airplane's radio: Hello, is this Paris, France? Come in, Paris France. Come in!

This is PARIS FRANCE! I spoke, desperately. Who are you? Repeat: Who are you?

I am Charles Lindbergh and I am flying The Spirit of Saint Louis, my airplane, and I am crossing the Atlantic Ocean and setting a record and I am coming to see you!

Charles LINDBERGH! I shouted: Come ahead, we know of you! Our country awaits you!

Rummm ummm.

I looked through the windscreen, and there it was! Brittany! Normandy? Our plane dropped altitude and we went in fast over farms and houses and yards and animals and people and the people looked up at us and we waved down to them but they didn't wave back because they were puzzled.

Radio in, I said to Lindy.

Is this Paris France? he cried, into the mike.

This is Paris France, I answered, and we await you. (We laughed.)

It was getting dark (which it wasn't).

This is Paris France awaiting you! In approaching darkness the landing field is lighted and ready!

This is Charles Lindbergh! I am coming in!

Lindy, he said, we're getting closer. We were both Lindy. *Then it was night.*

The crowd at the airfield was huge, and every eye searched the sky, and every ear heard Lindy's messages, as our radio was connected with the airport loudspeakers, which was the part we liked best, next to seeing the fisher-boats.

Look at those lights! I yelled. LINDY!

PARIS! Lindy shouted.

There's the landing strip! I pointed—look at all those *people!*

Lindy said, seriously, but with his eyes bright: Yes, Lindy! They're all French and they're waiting for us!

This is Lindy, are you there? he spoke into the mike.

We await you! I answered. PARIS FRANCE—We're going in!

Look, I said, intensely, they've made the landing strip like day!

Lindy nodded, and pulled the stick back. The plane rose, and then he banked it and we circled the field on a downward slant looking at all the people looking up at us, and we waved down and they cheered and waved back, as the searchlights followed us and we waved and circled the field.

My stomach felt more than funny.

Hallooo Paris, this is Lindy, I see you, and I'm coming in!

Come in, Lindy, we—I said weakly—we, eagerly await you!

The plane descended, lower and lower, and on a straight and even motion made a three-point landing, and in the forward thrust, as Lindy cried, We are here! I started to reply, but as the plane touched the field I jumped off the swing and vomited into the bushes while the plane taxied in and the crowd broke through the police lines. Lindy jumped out of the plane and ran to me, wide-eyed, then ran in the house and came back with his mom who told me to go home, rinse my mouth out, and lie down, which I did. But not before Lindy, who was as unhappy as I, asked what made me throw up? and after reasons etc., and it was all understood I'd come back later so we could greet the crowd and the press, his hat was buckled under his chin, he looked, to me, anyway, *like* Lindy, and I said it didn't matter, the altitude, bananas, sour milk, salt air, or the searchlights, and made my way home hoping nobody would be there to ask the rather obvious questions, and I was lucky, so I rinsed my mouth out, read another Big Little Book, *Kayo in The Land of Sunshine* (Florida), again, until I napped and woke when my sister came in, I felt great.

What! she cried: you in *bed?* It's past noon!

"I know," I said, happily. "I was sick."

She sat by me and I told her about the flight, and how the salt air got to me, and the suspense, and she began to laugh. Then we were sitting on my bed and both of us were laughing. Later I heard her tell Mommy in the kitchen and oh *boy* did *they* laugh!

Period.

. . . in heavy snowfall I walked up to and then across the east side of Kirkwood Road, bundled up in a kind of joy, as I sensed the thrill of the future pulling me toward Europe—albeit through the medium of the army—and after Europe, New York. I shuddered as I plunged through the heavy snow, and the thick dark evening Missouri cold

I shuddered too, in the force of her remembered embrace —her dark hair flowed down her naked body as she moved, lean young animal against me, black eyes full of questions, and her dusky healthy flesh its own perfume.

But she'd stayed on at the college, having decided not to go home for the holidays, so she could catch up with her work, in that quiet place in the mountains in western North Carolina. I envisioned her in her warm bed, reading, with her little lamp on, and curled amid her mess, while the Carolina wind came down the Blue Ridge mountains howling into the valley and shook the buildings.

I looked around me.

Velvet Freeze, there as always. But Kinkhorst's was closed, so was The National Cleaners, and in its place was a ladies' dress store, and beside it the new bookstore, owned by Elizabeth Wright, who sold the pamphlets I'd written and printed myself at school, in response to which the lovely lady from Cape Girardeau had written me my first fan letter, and Nancy Meyer had made the pamphlets front page news. Elizabeth Wright was a friend of my sister's—my sister who had married in 1947, and had moved to Glendale. Uncle Charley and family had moved to Virginia, Aunty Katie and Mil were retired. Lee Jones, too, and Dave, Herb, and Nancy Meyer ran the paper. Uncle Mouse and Frances got married in 1945, and moved to their dream house on top of a high hill in the country, west of Kirkwood. They had designed, and supervised, the building of their house, had planted trees, bushes, and flower beds, and made a garden, a grape arbor, and built a gazebo-arbor, where they sat in the warm afternoons and evenings until the mosquitoes got too fierce. On a clear day they could see into St. Louis.

They had called their land *Essex Field*.

Steve's mom had died in a plane crash, and as Jan had married and was on the West Coast (so was Steve), with Hobey in Europe continuing his work for MIT, their father sold the house and moved east. I didn't know where the Lizard, Wimp, and Cissie were, their folks were still on Long Island. . . .

The drifts were building, and the temperature was just this side of true cold. The air was still, no breeze at all, and in my scarf, cap, gloves, and zipper jacket, I was warm and happy. The snowflakes were big, and fat, and on my naked fingertip (having removed my glove) the macrocosmic snowflake was a microcosmically intricate and astonishing design.

Those big fat flakes fell slowly, like tiny white leaves, and covered Kirkwood and the Midwest beyond, with a soft clean white blanket, which was thickening, and getting very deep. The storm had begun that morning.

My Aunty Dorf and I had needed more tinsel for the tree, and I had gone down to Woolworth's for it, and was heading back.

I approached Adams Avenue, with the Presbyterian church on my right, the exact scene of the streetcar accident, nine years before.

Christmas music came from the church, and gave me a chill of love. I looked to the left at the clock on the bank, and envisioned the streetcar pulling up.

Cars drove slowly. I heard a clank of chains. That afternoon the city of Kirkwood had sent trucks out to spread cinders, and, in fact, I became aware that there was a truck to my left, and just behind me, and I saw two men spreading cinders, but in the heavy snowfall, and approaching night, the darkness being dense, I couldn't see them, or anything, actually, very clearly. The snow was almost translucent, as each flake reflected each other flake, like tiny bright faces, and this was really true in the country: the eerie, mystical glow deep in night when snowflakes reflect as they fall, tiny faces, heaven-sent winter fireflies, softly falling, falling as softly as pure thought.

I looked across Adams at the dark bulk of John Pitman, which looked so much smaller, and it had been so big.

I listened, and began to see something. Far away. Through the snow.

A shout came through, then another, and I looked around, not able to place it. Then I heard a bright and friendly laugh and I turned. A figure jumped down from the truck, and walked rapidly toward me.

Fee! he cried—*Fee Dawson!* The friendship caught my breath—Cecil! I said, and we laughed, took off our gloves and shook hands, exchanged greetings, our faces flushed and bright, reflecting faces, as the vapor from our parted lips made clouds, So GOOD to see you, so GREAT! to *see* you—

C'mon Davis, a gruff voice shouted, and the truck began to move. Cecil and I looked at each other. I asked, quickly —How are you? Are things—

I'm okay! he laughed, stepping back, Yes, things are okay! I heard you were writing and had a couple of books in the bookstore! he cried, jubilantly adding:

I heard you're in college. Like it? I bet you do!

I stepped forward, knowing things weren't okay, and not knowing what to say, except to know that he would without hesitation turn truth around to not touch this meeting, generous as always, and I said, about my college—Yes, I love it, but will be drafted soon.

The rough voice complained from the truck again, and Cecil turned and shouted that he was coming, turned to me and grinned, and standing just away from me, I saw his bright and eager eyes in a blur of straw blonde hair, as he asked, to the near tears in my eyes,

Are you still painting—writing, and painting?

I nodded in commitment, and said, Yes, I'm giving—I'm going to give my life to it.

He said, Gee that's swell, Fee—Good luck! he cried, and we took a step to each other, we briefly took each other's hands, and then he turned, ran to the truck, and clambered up, turned again and waved through the snowfall, calling —Be seein' ya! as I cried after him—

Be seein' ya!

Cecil!

Tiger Lilies

for you, *Cecil Davis*

Baseball, Mandalay, blueberries: in your memory.

October 1972–August 1976

New York/Vancouver

Fielding Dawson was born in 1930 in New York City. He grew up in Kirkwood, Missouri, attended Black Mountain College from 1949 to 1953, served in the United States Army from 1953 to 1955, and now writes and paints in New York City. Among his other books are the *Penny Lane* series and *Krazy Kat & 76 More,* his collected short stories.